Michele —

You are seriously

cool !

Geoff

Advance Praise for
Step Into The Spotlight!™

"Step Into The Spotlight! *is a necessary and delightful book. Necessary, because in today's world it's 'Distinct or Extinct.' Delightful because treating business and your career as show business is a heck of a lot more fun than approaching work as a cubicle slave performing a dreaded necessity.*"
Tom Peters, co-Author, *In Search of Excellence*

"*Since whatever you are marketing, including yourself, is a battle for the mind of your audience, this book cuts to the chase. Getting noticed is everything; not getting noticed is oblivion. It's must reading.*"
Jack Trout, co-Author, *Positioning*

"*We live in a celebrity-driven world and Tsufit tells you how to take advantage of that fact. Read this book to turn yourself into another Donald Trump or Richard Branson.*"
Al Ries, co-Author, *The Origin of Brands*

"*It takes a star to teach a star and it takes a star to want to learn stardom. Tsufit supplies half of what you need. If you can supply the other half, I'll see your name in starlight.*"
Jay Conrad Levinson, The Father of Guerrilla Marketing, Author, *Guerrilla Marketing* Series

"Step Into The Spotlight! *is an extraordinary book! It's an excellent guide to help people stand out from the crowd that no entrepreneur should be without!*"
Ivan Misner, Ph.D., Founder BNI and Author, *The World's Best Known Marketing Secret*

"Step Into The Spotlight! *is sparkling, dynamic and packed with practical hands-on advice. Bravo!*"
Sheldon Bowles, co-Author, *Raving Fans*

"Step Into The Spotlight! *distills the complexity of marketing and promotion down to one profoundly simple idea: How can you sell to them unless you can get them to stop on your channel? With her trademark humor, Tsufit delivers the secrets to capture and hold your audience's attention. This book is as captivating and dynamic as the author herself! Devour this book!*"

Raymond Aaron, co-Author, *Chicken Soup for the Canadian Soul*

"*Perhaps like you, Tsufit has a good case to make. But, knowing that simply having a good case is not enough, she shows us how to make our good case well. We'd be fools not to pay close attention.*"

Robert B. Cialdini, Ph.D., Author, *Influence: Science and Practice*

"*Tsufit's book is brilliant! All business IS show business. Don't let Tsufit's entertaining style fool you. This is the real stuff! Every page bursts with wonderful ideas to attract a following. A must read for any entrepreneur, speaker, author or anyone in business! Run, don't walk, to buy a copy of this book!*"

Dottie Walters, co-Author, *Speak And Grow Rich*

"*I love this book! Tsufit is a rare and refreshing new voice in business. And she hits the nail right on the head. Being great at what you do is not enough. If you want to be a success, become a star. This book shows you how.* Step Into The Spotlight! *should be required reading at Business Schools across the country. If you read only one new book this year, make it this one!*"

Bill Bartmann, Entrepreneur, Author, *Billionaire Secrets to Success*

"*Getting attention used to mean buying expensive advertising. Tsufit shows you a better way: Be a star so that people line up at your door!*"

David Meerman Scott, Author, *The New Rules of Marketing and PR*

"...*Tsufit's* Step Into The Spotlight! *is a must-read for every aspiring or seasoned professional. She reveals her secrets for success with mind-blowing strategies and networking techniques that will take everyone's career to a new level. Tsufit's writing style makes* Step Into The Spotlight! *a pleasurable read. Because of her proven methods, I will be using several tactics for my career."*

Les Brown, Internationally Renowned
Motivational Speaker

"Tsufit's book is phenomenal! Step Into The Spotlight! *takes business out from behind the desk and onto the stage. That's where the money is. I give this book a standing ovation!"*

Rick Frishman, co-Author, *Guerrilla Publicity*

"Tsufit's Step Into The Spotlight! *is a must for any business owner who wants to add some 'star power' to his or her business. Full of insightful and easy-to-implement tips, tricks and insider secrets guaranteed to help make you (and your business) famous!"*

Jordan McAuley, Author, *The Celebrity Black Book*

"Step Into The Spotlight! *just bursts and brims with energy, wisdom and a stellar call to action. WOW! Whether you are an entrepreneur building a business or an employee managing your career, you'll find wonderful ideas in this book. And you will have FUN reading it!"*

Susan RoAne, Author, *How To Work A Room*®

"Step Into The Spotlight! *is Fresh! Outrageous! And Bang On! ... One cannot help but be swept up in Tsufit's enthusiasm for showing the average entrepreneur how to walk onto the business stage and be a star! Buy this book now and watch your star rise."*

Raleigh Pinskey, Author, *101 Ways to Promote Yourself*

"Tsufit's book addresses what most people crave...Stardom. Whether it is attention to a recent media interview, release of a new product or new position in a rising career — we want the positive buzz to be around us. Finally the steps and tips to lead us to our own award winning performance are in print for the world to read and master."
Jamie Bright Forman, Network Television Producer

"Step Into The Spotlight! *is the best explanation of the most important skill for a small business owner: the ability to see what you're doing from the other person's point of view! Highly recommended."*
Derek Sivers, President, CD Baby

"Anyone can get caught up trying to compete in the 'noise' as Tsufit so elegantly explains. It is real easy to fall into the trap of trying to be heard by making more noise — but what we learn is that it's not any noise but the right noise and that's what makes this book worthwhile reading for any one who is serious about success."
Barry Siskind, Author, *Bumblebees Can't Fly*

"Whether you sell out to a large publisher or publish yourself, the author must do the promotion. The challenges are getting noticed and making your appearance fascinating, useful and memorable. This book shows the way."
Dan Poynter, Author, *The Self-Publishing Manual*

"If you're having trouble marketing yourself, you can learn how to step into the spotlight by reading this book. It's time for you to take center stage."
John Kremer, Author, *1001 Ways to Market Your Books*

STEP INTO THE
SPOTLIGHT!™

'Cause ALL Business Is Show Business!

A Guide to Getting Noticed

Tsufit

BEACH VIEW BOOKS

© 2008 TSUFIT

Published by Beach View Books
www.beachviewbooks.com

ISBN: 978-0-9781913-0-6
First Printing

Printed in Canada

Library and Archives Canada Cataloguing in Publication

Tsufit
    Step into the spotlight! — 'Cause ALL business is show business! :
    A guide to getting noticed / Tsufit.

Includes index.
ISBN 978-0-9781913-0-6

1. Marketing. 2. Business communication. 3. Communication in marketing.
I. Title.

HF5415.T74 2008   658.8   C2007-907643-2

To the four brightest stars in my life,
Daniela, Paloma, Riviera and Aviva.

And to my parents.
(Who've given me some of my best material.)

COMING ATTRACTIONS!

TABLE OF CONTENTS

CHAPTER 5   187

"Extra, Extra, Read All About It!" or
How To Get Your Face in the Newspaper
Without Robbing a Bank!
—THE POWER OF PUBLICITY

CHAPTER 6   247

"Everybody's a Critic!"
—THE SHOW MUST GO ON!

CHAPTER 7   257

Step Into The Spotlight!
—LIGHTS, CAMERA, ACTION! IT'S SHOWTIME!

INTRODUCTION

I'm thinking of making this book available in a plain brown wrapper. Or maybe giving it a fake book jacket with the title "Migratory Patterns of Birds".

'Cause truth be known, most people would rather be caught buying a porno flick than a book like this. Or a book I saw recently at the bookstore called *Brag*. It's crass and embarrassing to self promote, to toot your own horn, to seek fame and attention. Isn't it?

People are shy, not only about actually stepping into the spotlight, but even about admitting that they want to.

Maybe it's time for a new perspective on this. If you ask most people why they're doing what they're doing, some will admit they want to become multi-kazillionaires, but most say, "I just want to help people. I want to make a difference."

But how are you ever going to reach the people you want to help if they've never heard of you, if they don't know you exist?

> *"You can't save souls in an empty church."*
> Advertising Guru, David Ogilvy

It's not crass to want to attract enough clients to earn a living or to have the life you want. It's not shallow to make a name for yourself so that the people who need your help can find you. Once *you've* stepped into the spotlight, you can go out and help others do the same.

• • •

As an actress and singer, I've read many books about the business aspects of show business, books aimed at getting actors and singers to understand that there's more to the profession than "Let's Put on a Show in a Barn". It never occurred to me that, one day, I'd be writing a book for business about the lessons that can be learned from showbiz.

• • •

I watched a lot of TV growing up. In fact, I consider it one of my greatest learning experiences. I graduated, top of my class, from the "19-inch Institute of Higher Learning".

I always wanted to be a star! But it wasn't a direct route to stardom...

I went to law school, made the Dean's List, and then did the biggest show of my life. For ten years, I played the part of a lawyer in the smash hit show "Tsufit Goes to Bay St." (Kinda like those *Legally Blonde* movies, only without the pink Gucci briefcase.) I also took the lead in: "Four Kids in Four Years: The Musical".

One day, I thought, "There's gotta be more to life than this", so I made a monumental decision. I left the law, kept the kids, and decided to follow my dream of being a singer and a television actress.

My parents were predictably thrilled. "You're leaving law to be a *what*? Actress, Shmactress!" But I did it anyway. I left law for the limelight. I left business for show business.

I performed at comedy clubs, amphitheaters, played an evil cafeteria lady on a TV show for four years, did standup comedy on national TV, did commercials here and in Europe and released a music CD, *Under the Mediterranean Sky*.

People wanted to know how I'd made the move from lawyer to comedian and singer, how I made the transition and how I got so much attention. So it got me thinking...

I've been on stage all my life. For me, getting noticed has never been a problem. In high school, in university... Boy, did I have *chutzpah* in university! (More about *chutzpah* in Chapter 2). By the ripe old age of 19, I had asked Donald Sutherland out to lunch, country singer Carol Baker if I could be her backup singer and Joan Rivers if I could be on her TV show. I sang and acted in live shows across the country all through university, highlighting my textbooks between scenes.

So, it wasn't so much a transition, as a return to my natural state. But still people wanted advice on how to "be a star". They asked me to coach them. So I did.

I show business how to use show business to get business.

When attending business functions, I found I was an instant hit. I got attention. And clients. What was my secret, everyone wanted to know? How did I attract clients with just a 30 second *shpiel*?

Well I guess all those years of performing, both on stage and in court, paid off. I applied what I learned as an entertainer to my business.

Now, I show business how to use show business to get business.

● ● ●

I inhale books. I buy them, pile them and read them, 8-10 at a time. I have more books than the average metropolitan library. And, like a musician is influenced by the music she listens to, I'm sure that I've absorbed many of the ideas I've read. They mix with my own, I add a few stories and they become, or so I think, my ideas. It would be impossible to go back and individually thank all the authors for their contributions, mostly because I don't know who said what. This used to really bother me until I started noticing that many of the books I read also borrow from each other.

In the words of Mark Twain, *"What a good thing Adam had. When he said a good thing, he knew nobody had said it before."*

If you find some of your brilliance in this book, know that I thank you, honor you and acknowledge you here. (i.e., Don't sue me!)

Now, let's get started. The spotlight awaits.

C H A P T E R 1

Getting Them
to Stop on Your
Channel

GETTING NOTICED

*I*t's noisy out there!

You're an entrepreneur and you want to shout it from the rooftops. But how can you get anyone to listen? It's like your prospects have a television remote and they're flicking through the channels to see what's on. You hope it's you. But sometimes it feels like you're stuck on Channel 632.

We're living in an "overcommunicated" society. Consumers are on information overload. That's what marketing gurus, Al Ries and Jack Trout, told us in their ground-breaking book, *Positioning*. And that was back in 1981, before the Internet, before hundreds of cable channels, before advertising embedded in the supermarket floor tiles and conveyor belts, before talking subway posters and before the world went wireless.

We exist in a world of instant everything, from faxes to e-mail, from instant messaging to text messaging. And all the noise makes it more and more confusing for prospects to sort through it all. The result? It's harder and harder to get an audience's attention.

Bored audiences are temporarily shocked out of their stupor with "reality" television but even bug eating contests get old after a while. Nowadays, even *My Big Fat Ugly Bungee-Jumping Lesbian Siamese Twin Grandmother's Full Body Makeover* wouldn't shock or attract many viewers.

So How Do You Get Them to Stop on Your Channel?

And even if you do get them to stop, how long will they stay there? I remember watching *The Jetsons* as a kid and marveling at a world of moving sidewalks, robots and instant food. On *Get Smart*, secret agent Maxwell Smart had a telephone in his shoe. Big deal. Now, that phone can fit into his pocket and take pictures. He can even watch TV on it. Or download music. Or send an e-mail to a farmer in Mozambique.

You can't shout your way to success.

The result of living in the fast lane is that we have very little patience. A second or two and if you haven't grabbed us, Bam! We've switched the channel on you.

> *The human mind deals with clutter the best way it can — by blocking most of it out.*
> Marty Neumeier, *Zag*

Shouting contests between well bankrolled advertisers aren't the answer. You can't shout your way to success. You have to find a way to break through the invisibility barrier, to take center stage and become the star of your own show.

My Story
•••••••••••

OK. So, the watching TV part, you know. When the Nielsen TV Ratings people were facing a deadline and the viewer results weren't all in yet, they'd just pick up the phone, and ask, "Hey, Tsufit. Whatdya think?"

My Dad's a Math Professor. My Mom? Professor of Everything. So for me, they had big expectations. My Dad wanted me to become a doctor and find a cure for cancer. My Mom wanted me to marry a doctor and find a good dining room set.

But me, I just wanted to be a star! So I performed on the backyard deck and watched TV, all the educational shows — *Gilligan's Island, I Dream of Jeannie, The Beverly Hillbillies, Bewitched.* I did get an amazing education. 4 P.M. Sharp! Every day. It was a pretty rigorous programme back then. In those days, you actually had to get up off the couch to change channels. Manually!

As you now know, I didn't become a doctor. My dining room set? A pine table and six white plastic patio chairs. But I did get on TV. Some shows, some commercials. Nothing fancy. Let's just say, *fresh produce* was usually involved... And you know the rest.

As I came to be noticed by the media and by the crowds, people started asking me how I did it. Next thing you know, I'm a coach, coaching entrepreneurs (and assorted other business types) to get noticed! No marketing degree, no coaching certification, and still they come!

Now, I make my living from what I learned from that box. Forget "thinking outside the box". Why would you? Everything you need to know is right in there! *In* the box.

It was years later, when I started attending business functions, that it dawned on me. People who had been attending these things for years asked what my secret was, how I attracted new clients so quickly.

One day, I had an epiphany. I realized that the reason I was attracting was because instinctively I knew that *ALL business is show business*!

There it was, a formula for success in business that even entrepreneurs with MBAs and PhDs didn't know. And it was only by being in both worlds that I recognized it.

ALL Business is show Business.

Now, I'm on a mission to bring color to business, by helping entrepreneurs and "the suits" to step into the spotlight and get noticed. You've probably figured it out by now — I subscribe to the "We're All Entrepreneurs" theory of business. So yes, this book *is* for you.

I'm particularly well suited to my career. Why?

1) I'm naturally very snoopy,

2) I love to critique (Heck, I do it for free!),

3) I love to tell people what to do,

4) I've got this built in "bore-ometer" that scientifically measures levels of boredom, the "yawn factor", in people's speeches.

But mostly, because…

5) I love treasure hunting. I love finding a diamond in the rough and making it sparkle.

So that's what I do. I dig for the buried treasure in my clients. I find it, polish it and show them how to show-case it, publicize it and take it to market.

And I'm here to tell all.

There's No Business Like Show Business!

In 1946, Irving Berlin wrote a song "There's No Business Like Show Business" for the musical *Annie Get Your Gun*. Great show. Great song. But Irv was wrong. *All* business is show business.

No one knows how to capture and hold an audience's attention better than entertainers. This book will show you how to get your act together and take it on the road.

More and more businesses are starting to see the connection. Entire firms of lawyers are sent to study with comedy improvisation troupes. Donald Trump added a Hollywood production company to his business empire. Companies like Roots, Planet Hollywood and the Hard Rock Cafe understand the power of business' association with showbiz, and it shows in their success.

So, how do *you* get into show business?

Getting the Audition

Till you get your name up in lights, you'll have to audition for business. And as every actor knows, the toughest part of the process is not the audition itself, it's getting into the audition, getting past the battle-axe with the horn-rimmed glasses, convincing her that you really are on her list, even though she can't find your name or your 8 × 10 glossy anywhere. How can you show them your stuff, how can you dazzle them, if you can't get your 15 seconds on the audition room floor?

Many entrepreneurs are corporate escapees and the only way they know how to attract business is based on the corporate model. Buy a suit, rent an office, print some stationery and have some power lunches at the old boys' club. Replacing that model with a showbiz model will put your business on the marquee.

If you learn this stuff well enough, one day you won't have to audition. The scripts will be sent to you.

That doesn't mean no one will ever ask you to prove yourself. It just means you won't have to agree to do it. Rumor has it that, late in her career, actress Shelley Winters was asked to come in and read for a role in a movie. She walked into the audition room, sat down, pulled an Oscar statuette out of her purse, then pulled out another one and said, "Some people in this town think I can act." She then put her Oscars back in her bag and walked out.

Whether you're an entrepreneur, a CEO or somewhere in between, isn't it time you learn how to step into the spotlight and star in your business?

Don't End Up on the Cutting Room Floor!

I say that as someone who's been there, literally. OK, so I was just an extra, but I was still really excited about seeing myself on the big screen in the Richard Burton movie. Either I blinked and missed it or I ended up on the cutting room floor. Don't let that happen to you.

How can you make sure you don't get edited out of the scene? By stepping into the spotlight and being so capti-vating they won't be able to edit you out. By stealing the scene. This book will show you how.

• • •

Chambers of Boredom
....

By way of intro, I gotta confess, I don't do boring very well! And being one of those "Emperor's Got No Clothes" kinda chicks, I can't even fake it!

So when I go to these Chamber of Commerce Networking Breakfasts (they don't call them the "Bored of Trade" for nothing) and I find myself stuck between an accountant in a grey suit and a financial planner in a blue suit, I'm thinking, "If one of these guys spilled some scrambled egg on his lapel, at least it'd add a dash of color!"

Many entrepreneurs like to say "I'm a one man show." But they often don't realize how very true that is. It *is* a show. Initially, you play all the parts both on stage and off. You're the director, producer and star. But too many entrepreneurs spend too much time as stage hands, backstage, preparing and perfecting. The show itself becomes an afterthought, if a thought at all. So, your audience wanders off in search of a more compelling show and another business bites the dust.

Ever wonder why the failure rate for new businesses is so high? It's not that entrepreneurs aren't committed. It's not that they aren't hard workers. But they're suffering from a fundamental misconception. Most entrepreneurs naively think that being great at what they do is enough. It's not! It never was.

Being Great Gets You to Zero, Not Above
....

A reviewer from *Billboard* magazine once told me that he really liked my music, but that my CD wasn't "on the radar screen" and that he wasn't going to review it. At that time, I had no idea what that expression meant. Now I do.

Making it in today's overcrowded marketplace depends less on *baking a better bagel* and more on *branding it.*

Talent is only the starting point.
Irving Berlin

Of course it's important to be great at what you do.

You can't brand crap.
Guy Kawasaki, *The Art of the Start*

It's crucial, but it's *not* enough to get you noticed. It's not enough to get you "on the radar". It doesn't matter what you do or how well you do it, unless someone knows about it.

An "expert" is not someone who knows what he knows. An expert is someone who is *known* for knowing what he knows. And therein lies the rub.

> An "expert" is not someone who knows what he knows. An expert is someone who is known for knowing what he knows.

Stand In or Stand Out

It's time to step out of the shadows. In the movies, a "stand-in" is basically a body, a place holder, someone roughly the size of the lead actor who's hired to stand on a mark for hours while the camera crew adjusts the lighting and sets up the shot. No one will ever know the stand-in's name or ever see him on screen. The camera is pointed in his direction but the film isn't rolling. In some ways, he's invisible. His whole job is just to stand there, so the star can relax in his dressing room sipping margaritas. The stand-in is

12

totally replaceable and disposable once the star walks onto the set.

I once saw a cute film called *Pipe Dream* about a plumber who pretends to be a movie director in order to get "seen". He complains that when people see him, they see only a plumber, a service person, but not him. Testing his theory about the invisibility of categories of people, he challenges his friend in a restaurant to describe their waitress. The friend can't. Like the plumber, the waitress isn't noticed. The plumber thinks this is an affliction of the working class, the blue collars.

But it doesn't matter what color your collar is. It's exactly the same for real estate agents, insurance brokers, accountants, IT consultants, financial planners. And it's not just "the suits". Web designers, health and wellness professionals…you're not being "seen".

In the film, the plumber makes up a persona as a film director and all of a sudden, his world becomes glamorous. He gets noticed and he becomes the subject of industry buzz. Next thing you know, he's in demand.

As the film progresses, he gets called out to do an emergency plumbing job for an old client. The client's husband is an agent who had been wooing him when he was posing as a film director. The plumber is worried about being busted. But there's no danger of that. He isn't recognized by the husband even when the agent pays him because, once again, no one notices "the plumber".

So how do you turn yourself from a plumber into a producer?

Seduce the Spotlight!
••••••••••••••••••••••••

One thing we know from movies and TV news is that what gets seen is whatever the camera is pointed at. The fact that something exists, doesn't mean it'll get picked up on camera.

What's the point of performing your show outside the spotlight? It's like winking in the dark, as the saying goes. What's the point? No one can see you.

We have to learn to seduce the spotlight. And once we get the camera pointed in our direction, we need to know how to keep it there.

Making it depends less on baking a better bagel and more on branding it.

In business, as in show business, there's no show unless there's an audience. Actors know that you can be in rehearsal for a show for six months, but if there's no audience on opening night, the show closes. Many businesses still haven't figured this out.

When I was a young lawyer, I naively thought that if I just did great work, I'd be a huge success. And I did great work. But when the recession hit and the rainmakers stopped making rain, they turned to the worker bees and said, "It's your turn. Go out and get some clients."

How do you get 'em? The way I see it, you have two choices. Sign up for "Prospecting 101" and spend the rest of your life making cold calls *or* step into the spotlight and become a star.

The Department of Chutzpah

ATTITUDE IS EVERYTHING!

It's unbelievable how many people choose to be in the background, an extra, in the audience, in the chorus...

Nothing wrong with playing a supporting role, but isn't that what a *job* is? Didn't you become an entrepreneur to be a star?

Which would you rather be? Batman or Robin? You know Robin's never going to get his own show.

Which would you rather be? Batman or Robin? You know Robin's never going to get his own show.

THE ART OF ATTRACTION

*S*tars are different. They stand out. Most people have star potential, but don't let themselves shine. Which makes it easy pickin's for the rest of us.

The best way to be a star is to be yourself. This is actually pretty rare nowadays. Everyone is trying to fit in, to conform. Fuggedaboutit!

We have to *unlearn* a bunch of stuff. Stuff like dressing and speaking and acting the way we think we're supposed to — to look "professional". But most importantly, we have to learn not to "cut to the chase".

Don't Cut to The Chase!
••••••••••••••••••••••••••••••••

Imagine you're walking down the street, minding your own beeswax, thinking about how you can get your own reality TV series, when, all of a sudden, out of the blue, someone starts chasing you!

What do you do? You run. But, he catches you, by the arm. What do you do now? You struggle! You try to get away! Natural instinct, right?

Too many entrepreneurs are chasers. They chase their potential customers with cold calls, and e-mails and faxes.

And what do their prospects do? They try to escape! No one likes to be caught! It's dopey. Because what works is exactly the opposite.

Business is a seduction.

Can you imagine a theater troupe chasing people down the street to get an audience? When's the last time you got a cold call from Madonna?

Cold Calls Leave You Cold?

I'm not saying cold calls don't work. They do. But cold calling is chasing. Cold calls diminish the caller and creep out the "callee". They're an intrusion. They're uncomfortable and they're unnecessary.

If you learn the art of attraction, throw in a little bit of showbiz, you'll never have to make another cold call again.

So, how *do* you get them into the theater?

Viva Las Vegas!

True Story. After I'd only been a lawyer for about 10 minutes my new firm whisks us all off to Las Vegas for a four day retreat. (Now you know why legal fees are what they are.) I walk into a casino, first time in my life, and see this woman in a beautiful sparkly top. And, I like sparkly things, so I walk up to her: "Hey Lady. Can I buy your beautiful sparkly top?" Four days later, I'm standing on stage at a comedy club in Toronto, wearing the beautiful sparkly top.

What's the point of the story? The point is that *I* was the buyer and yet *I* initiated the sale. Why? Because I was attracted to it. Because it sparkled!

That's the way I conduct my business. I do my best to sparkle in public and then let people come to *me*. I let them come ask if they can buy from me.

Today, most products and services are *bought* not *sold*. We have no patience for the Willy Lomans or the used car salesmen of the world.

> *Marketing is not the art of selling. It's not the*
> *simple business of convincing someone to buy. It is*
> *the art of creating conditions by which the buyer*
> *convinces himself.*
>
> Harvey Mackay, *Swim with the Sharks*

We'll decide what we want and when and where we'll buy it. The most you can hope to do is attract us.

And it won't take us long to decide.

In the Blink of an Eye

In his fascinating book, *Blink*, Malcolm Gladwell shares the results of studies that show how quickly and accurately we form impressions. In one study, university students were shown three 10 second video clips of teachers in the classroom with the sound off. They were asked, based on that brief snippet of information, to rate the teachers' effectiveness. Amazingly enough, their evaluations were remarkably similar to evaluations submitted by actual students who attended classes for the full semester.

And the bizarre thing is that I decided to read *Blink* based on a 3 second encounter. I was waiting for a client in a book store and the book caught my eye. Of course, I wouldn't have seen it if someone hadn't placed it face outwards, but the short name and understated layout were enough to captivate me and pull me inside. After a paragraph, I was hooked. That's all it takes.

It gets weirder. My client arrives and I tell her, all excited, about this fantastic book I just picked up. She tells me that she told me about that book last week. Not only that, but she claims to have given me an Internet review of the book that I put in my file. I sheepishly open the folder. Sure enough, there it is.

I hadn't heard her. She tried to sell me on the book but I hadn't heard a word or even looked at whatever she handed me. I didn't even have a memory of her mentioning it. Whatever she said didn't attract me. I ended up discovering the book myself.

Don't Just Sit on the Shelf!

I'm not suggesting that you just sit there like that book. We've all heard the story of Lana Turner sitting on a stool at a soda fountain and next thing you know, she's a big movie star. Bruce Willis was discovered while tending bar in New York City. But it doesn't usually work like that.

Too many entrepreneurs are content to just sit on the shelf, like a loaf of white bread, and wait to be picked. But they don't give people any reason to pick them!

So they wait longer, 'cause everyone tells them "It takes five years to get a new business off the ground".

No, it doesn't! Let me tell you, that bread doesn't get any sexier after five years sitting on the shelf.

You have to learn how to attract your audience. If you do, you'll never have to make another cold call again. Ever. I don't.

"You Had Me at 'Hello'"

I got a call from a company in Connecticut. The guy wanted me to train his sales team in Canada. I asked him how he heard of me. He said he'd been in Canada a year earlier and saw me at an event. I asked if I was the speaker. He said "No. You just did your 30 seconds."

30 Seconds! Remembered me. Called me. Hired me. A year later. No cold call, no warm call, no "fax me your proposal". Just hired me. That's the power of knowing how to step into the spotlight.

Remember that scene in *Jerry Maguire* when the Tom Cruise character delivers his passionate declaration of love for the girl? Several minutes into it, Renée Zellweger tells him: "You had me at 'hello'."

So how can you attract new clients in just 30 seconds? We'll talk specifics in Chapter 4. But first, we need an approach. We've said "no" to cold calls, "no" to chasing, but we also know that we can't sit there like a loaf of white bread (the "Bake It and They Will Come" approach). So what's left? At this point, some entrepreneurs might resort to putting on a "dog and pony show", some elaborate spectacle to get attention.

Get Discovered!
....

Futurist, Faith Popcorn, offers an interesting alternative. Popcorn observes that women don't like an overly aggressive marketing approach and suggests we "Market to Her Peripheral Vision". It's a fabulous idea, and not just for marketing to women. We're all sick of the noise.

So how can you market to your prospects' peripheral vision? It's a classic B movie maneuver — you know the one, where the girl dances with a handsome stranger to make her boyfriend jealous. Cousin to the only marginally more sophisticated "Get the Best Friend to Like You" move demonstrated by Will Smith to his dating protégés in the movie *Hitch*. Cheesy, but they work.

Allow Your Audience to Discover You
....

When you want to get noticed, aim your show at the people *near* your target instead of tap dancing directly in your target's face.

You gotta be subtle or it can backfire. Big time! We're not going for court jester here. Too obvious and it's a real "turn off". But it's a risk worth taking. Nine times out of ten, when properly executed, it works. You get noticed. "Fresh baked apple pie on the window sill" noticed.

I save this maneuver for situations where the person I want to notice me is famous or the star of the evening and a direct approach would make me look like just another autograph hound.

The Side Show
....

I mount a side show somewhere within my target's peripheral vision and entertain a few unsuspecting audience members. Sometimes my targets come over and join the crowd. Other times they just take note and approach me later, sometimes even months later. But they're hooked. And it's not my job to reel them in. They've been caught in my magnetic field. And then it's just a matter of time.

We all value what we discover ourselves. Allow your audience to "discover" you.

BEING A STAR IS AN ATTITUDE

Attitude is Everything!

*N*ot ready to put on a side show?

To be a star, you gotta have *"chutzpah"*.

A client asked me recently what it means. I don't have an exact definition. But my mom always says I have it and, as you probably realize by now, my mom is always right.

Chutzpah is attitude in its most concentrated, potent, undiluted form. (By the way, if you don't spit on the person in front of you when you say it, you're saying it all wrong.) It can be used for good or evil, but when properly directed, it can be the difference between being a star or an "also ran".

Chutzpah can't be bought, so you'll just have to grow some yourself. Not sure it's worth it?

It's worth it.

Just 5 minutes in front of the right audience can be worth more than a whole year behind your desk.
Quoted by Rob Sherman, *21 Laws of Speaking*

And the essential element is confidence.

Confidence Sells

After I graduated from law school, I went to 19 articling interviews. I had done well in school, so I was cocky and confidently told all of them I wanted an office with a big window, not the dinky little cubicles that were generally assigned to lowly articling students. I walked into the interviews with the attitude of a star. Tsufit was in the building!

I got my window. In my very own office. With my very own door.

High School Confident-ial

I was at my high school reunion years ago and I saw the older sister of one of the guys I had a crush on in school. So I went up to her and said "Hi. You don't know me (she was five years older than me), but I went to school with your brother. Is he here?"

She said: "Are you kidding? Of course, I know who you are. When we first moved into our house, you were about eight and you came over to us and said: 'Hi, I'm Tsufit, Welcome to the neighborhood!'"

But what if you don't have that kind of confidence?

Fake It Till You Make It!

Fake it! I know, I know, I said "Be yourself". I lied.

Be yourself. Only be the best version of yourself.

Applause

Years ago, I was auditioning for a local production of the musical *Applause*. Did the singing audition, did fine. Did the acting audition, did fine. Next came the dancing audition. Let's just say, dancing's not my forte.

> I was so confident, that I made the nine other good dancers think that they had the steps wrong!

So I'm on stage, me and nine other dancers, good dancers, *real* dancers, and I thought "What am I going to do?"

What *did* I do? I plastered a big confident smile on my face, held my head high, arms strong and confident in the air, and I danced! G-d only knows what I did from the waist down, but I gotta tell you, I was *so* confident, that I made the nine other good dancers think that *they* had the steps wrong!

And I got a callback for a lead role.

Not Good Enough for the Chorus? Be the Star!

You know who had *chutzpah*? Fanny Brice. Remember that movie, *Funny Girl*, where Barbra Streisand plays Fanny, an uncoordinated gawky wannabe chorus girl auditioning for the Zeigfeld Follies?

I learned a lot from that movie. Fanny wasn't good enough to be in the chorus. But she was good enough to be the star!

Crazy as it sounds, sometimes it's easier to be the star than to have to fit into the chorus. And you get to wear the Bob Mackie gown.

Step into the Spotlight!
....

You *are* good enough to be the star of your own business. But you have to step into the spotlight, or no one will ever know!

Have a Theme Song
....

OK, so this one is going to sound really dumb. I warned you. But it actually works.

Remember the TV show, *Ally McBeal*? John Cage, the quirky little litigator, used to pump up his confidence by imagining velvety voiced crooner Barry White singing while Cage danced in the co-ed bathroom. Often co-workers would feel the vibe and join in with him.

I had a client who regularly had to get up in front of hundreds of business women and she was often nervous and "not herself". I suggested that before getting on stage, she should dance backstage, across the floor, to her favorite music. I usually bop to my favorite Latin music while driving to my concert gigs. By the time I hit the stage, I'm pumped. I'm "on" and ready to captivate my audience.

For a hilarious but powerful example of what music can do for your confidence, check out the movie, *Keeping the Faith*, where Ben Stiller and Ed Norton play a rabbi and a priest strutting their holy stuff down the streets of Manhattan to the tune of Santana's "Smooth".

The key distinguishing factor between a successful person and someone who isn't often comes down to attitude. Confidence. Or at least, the appearance of confidence. Develop it. Or learn to fake it till you make it.

Remember, you are a star.

Razzle Dazzle 'Em
....

The key is to be yourself, only better! Be the best version of yourself!

Speaking of Babs, casting director Michael Shurtleff tells the story of auditioning a young Barbra Streisand for the role of Miss Marmelstein in *I Can Get It for You Wholesale* with producer David Merrick, Arthur Laurents and writer Jerome Weidman.

According to Shurtleff, Streisand walked in late, on the last day of auditions, wearing her raccoon coat and two mismatched shoes, explaining that she saw these wonderful shoes in a thrift shop, but only one of each pair fit. She was chewing gum while delivering this rapid monologue and then a few notes into her song summoned the stage hand to fetch her a stool. She started to sing another couple of notes and then took the gum out of her mouth and stuck it under the stool before wowing them with her voice. No one knew what to make of this "ugly", nutty girl with the spectacular voice. After the audition, they made an amazing discovery.

There was no gum under the stool! There never had been. It was all an act to stand out. And she did. She got the part.

Talk about *chutzpah!* Arthur Laurents remembers the 19 year old "neophyte": "She sat in the chair and interviewed us. It was like the Barbra Streisand talk show."

Kick It Up a Notch!
....

The first time I saw chef Emeril Lagasse on TV, I thought he was a comedian with a cooking show. Later, I saw a documentary about his start in the business. It showed clips of a standard cooking show with a standard delivery, nothing to sauté your onions. One day, in a stroke of genius, they stuck him in front of a live audience. All of a sudden, his comedic abilities (which had previously entertained only the crew between scenes) kicked in. And "Bam!" He "kicked it up a notch" and the rest is history.

Emeril has his own restaurants, his own line of grocery store products, even a run at a TV sitcom, all because he mixed showbiz with his chef biz.

Star Quality

You don't have to be suitable! If you're a star, you don't have to fit in! The world will make a place for you!

In high school, I auditioned for my first musical. By the time I got there, there was only one role left, a Mexican innkeeper named Manuel. They changed the role to Rosita and gave it to me.

Same thing happened when I was applying for my first job as a lawyer. They'd already offered the job to someone else 10 minutes earlier. After the head honcho met me, he called an emergency partner's meeting and added a second position, just so they could hire me.

You don't have to fit in. The world will make a place for you.

When Barbra auditioned for *I Can Get It for You Wholesale*, the only part available was the role of a 50-year-old spinster. The 19-year-old got the part. As Arthur Laurents said "Barbra knew she would be a star and she is." As a wise woman once said, if you've got star quality, you don't have to fit in. The world will make a place for you.

> You don't have to fit in. The world will make a place for you.

And if it doesn't, make a place for yourself. How? Like I said, "Fake it till you make it!"

The "It" Factor

In showbiz, there's an expression "You've got 'it'." What's "it"?

The reason they call it "it" is because it's hard to put it into words. It's got something to do with charisma, magnetism, the power to attract and hold an audience.

Can "it" be developed? Most people say "Either you got it or you don't".

I'm not sure whether that kind of presence, charisma, can be learned, planted where it totally doesn't exist. But I do know it can be awakened from the dead.

Access Your Inner Elvis

I just saw a movie about Elvis' life. Why are people so fascinated by Elvis? Me, I'm a huge Elvis fan. Why was the guy such a star? Was it his look, his personality, his voice, his music? It's probably all of those things — together with this magical thing called "it", the "it" factor. Elvis had "it". But even with Elvis, it took him a while to find his inner "it".

In the movie, a docu-drama (or shlock-u-drama), Elvis walks into Sun Records, a small Memphis recording studio, to sing for Sam Phillips. Elvis sings like Bill Monroe; he sings like Bing Crosby; he sings like yesterday's news. Just another singer. A dime a dozen.

It wasn't a quickie, even for Elvis, to find his original voice. But he kept at it and Phillips kept pushing him. Eventually he did find it. And the rest is history!

Don't be discouraged if it takes you a while to find your original voice and your confidence, your inner "it".

Like Elvis, like Emeril, chances are that, somewhere deep inside, you've got some "it". You just have to find it. This book will help you do just that.

Can You Ride a Horse?
....

Every actor knows that when the casting director asks "Can you ride a horse?" the correct answer, the only answer, is "yes". And then you high-tail it off to the stables to make it true.

I'm not suggesting entrepreneurs agree to do whatever they're asked to do. Nor is lying ever a good policy. But you can be creative in your response.

> *Never having seen a horse outside of the movies, he responded modestly, "Well of course, I'm not an expert," when asked about his riding abilities.*
> M. Newhouse and P. Messaline,
> *The Actor's Survival Kit*

The point is that by acting out the role of a success in business, you'll attract more success, real success. Before you know it, it becomes true.

And the truth is, many very successful entrepreneurs suffer from "fraud syndrome" even when, by all external measures, they're hugely successful. They're afraid that, one day, someone will walk into their Madison Avenue office tower and expose them as an imposter.

If you're going to feel like a fraud even when you make it to the top, why be humble now?

The Totem Pole
....

It's quite amusing to attend a showbiz industry party. Everyone's playing the game of "Totem Pole". It's an exercise where you try to figure out if the person you're talking to is more important or less important in the industry than you. If he's more important, you stick around, suck up, try to impress and pump him for information. If he's less important, you try to impress him while looking over his shoulder for someone more important to talk to. The measure of importance may have to do with how many projects he's done and with whom, how many contacts he has and whether he can help you get a leg-up or not.

The amusing part is in watching the participants try to find their relative spots on the pole. Kinda like a game of "rock, paper, scissors".

A: "So, who's your agent?" (His agent's better. Maybe he can introduce me. Great contact.)

B: "You played DeNiro's sidekick?" (He's famous. Three rungs down for me.)

A: "Yeah, I do a lot of stuff with the big guys." (No need for him to know it was a low budget horror flick and I was cut out of almost every scene.)

I spend a lot of time discussing the Totem Pole with clients. Where do you want to be on the Totem Pole? And how do you plan to get there?

Most of my clients don't have the time or patience to work their way up from the chorus. And why do that if it's not necessary? You're not 22 anymore.

Where you are on the Totem Pole is pretty much where you place yourself.

Be Willing to Walk
····························

I placed myself high on the Totem Pole when I first started my business. I charged a substantial consulting fee, I scheduled appointments according to the preset times that worked for me and I had clients come to me regardless of how far they came from or how well known they were. Most importantly, I held myself high.

I was willing to walk away from potential clients before I even had clients, if the set-up wasn't right for me. I knew that I was destined to be successful from day one and somehow managed to communicate that to others.

Carry yourself like a star and people will treat you that way.

She Who Glitters Gets the Gold
·············

As I'm writing this, dazzling fireworks just exploded outside my window. And I had to stop and look. Sparkle is irresistible.

> *How can you sell to them unless you can get them to stop on your channel?*

You know that expression "All that glitters is not gold"? That may be true, but it's equally true that she who glitters gets the gold. Don't be afraid to sparkle.

Remember, the goal is to get your audience's attention. How can you sell to them unless you can get them to stop on your channel?

CHAPTER 3

"I'm Ready For
My Close-Up,
Mr. DeMille"

ARE YOU BEING SEEN?

*O*ne of the biggest challenges any business faces is visibility, being seen in the crowd.

Entrepreneurs shell out big bucks for logos and letterhead, believing that this will create their "brand". It won't. Nice to have, but your brand isn't a spiffy logo.

You are your brand.

I'm not saying that logos aren't important. When my daughter, Daniela, was only two, she said "Mommy, Mommy, The Bay", correctly identifying the 300 year old Hudson's Bay Company only from its logo. But, logos alone ain't gonna get you there.

Ever see the reality TV show *Beauty & The Geek*? As I explained to my four teenage daughters, it's a show about branding. 8 "beauties" and 8 "geeks". Who decided which was which?

Your *brand* is your *audience's* perception of you. This chapter is about what you can do to shape, color and influence that perception.

BE YOUR OWN
CASTING DIRECTOR

Which Part Do You Want to Play?

*W*hen I was a kid, we'd all audition for the high school musical, sleep on pins and needles all night long, and then rush to school at 8 A.M. to see the Cast List posted on the front foyer wall. We all pushed and shoved to see it first and then spent the rest of the morning asking each other "Whatdya get?"

I was thrilled when I was cast in the role of Yente in *Fiddler on the Roof*, crushed when Anita in *West Side Story* went to a bleached blonde — didn't they know Anita was supposed to be a spunky brunette?

There Are No Small Parts, Only Small Actors

That's what they tell you in theater to encourage each actor to make something out of whatever role he's given. But as an entrepreneur, you have to consider very carefully whether you want a bit part or a lead.

Recently, I spent almost nine hours in the hospital emergency room with my daughter who had pneumonia.

My eldest daughter was there with us. "Look at those two women," I told her, indicating two very similar looking Asian women working the night shift. One was mopping the floors and the other was the star of the show, the doctor we had waited nine hours to see. My daughter thought I was minimizing the role of the woman mopping the floor. Not at all.

The orderly's role in the chorus, the job of keeping the hospital clean, is crucial, just as the doctor's role is crucial. The only difference is that almost anyone could play the orderly's role. Very few people can play the doctor's role. And for that difference, the doctor gets paid at least 10 times as much as the other woman and is treated, sadly, with 10 times the respect. Literally hundreds of people waited hour after hour after hour for the appearance of the star, the way autograph seekers and paparazzi wait for Brad Pitt. All we wanted was a few minutes with the star. Nobody noticed or applauded when the orderly put on a mask and gown and went to disinfect the triage room.

Star status is relative. It depends on what stage you're playing on and who else is on stage with you. I'm sure if Julia Roberts had stopped by the emergency room, even the doctor would have been pushed out of the limelight. The plumber, in the movie described earlier, may not have felt like a star, but on stage with a bunch of general handymen, he's a somebody, as I found out recently when I had to shell out 200 big ones to get one to fix the leak in our bathtub. I didn't ask the plumber about my broken fan in the kitchen the way I might have if he were a general handyman. It's understood the plumber has to rush out for his next show and we accept that, like we accept Tom Cruise not hanging around on the couch with other interview guests because he has to catch a plane to his movie set overseas. On the other hand, if

35

he wasn't available, any other plumber would have served the purpose.

Best Supporting Actor

Technicians and worker bees don't get the spotlight. Artists do. Experts do. Stars do. So you're going to have to make a choice. Which do you want to be?

For me, the answer is obvious. It took me a while to realize that not everybody feels that way.

The Spotlight is Not for Everyone

The roller coaster ride of stardom is not for everyone. If at a certain point you decide the spotlight is not for you, don't hesitate to put down this book and go back to your accounting practice.

But if you want to get known, if you want to stand out, if you want people to seek you out rather than having to hunt for business, keep reading.

> *My mother said to me, if you become a soldier, you'll be a general; if you become a monk, you'll end up as the pope. Instead, I became a painter and wound up as Picasso.*
>
> Pablo Picasso

A Painter or a Picasso?

I have a client who's an interior designer. She's quite quirky and eccentric herself, so I was surprised how hard she fought me when we discussed defining her style and her persona. She insisted that she had to give the customer

36

what he wanted; she had to be adaptable, flexible and therefore couldn't define her personal style. Makes sense for a business to give its customers whatever they want, right? Not as much sense as you think. That's a good approach if you simply want a good run in the chorus. But if you're seeking the spotlight, that approach will never get you there.

There are artists who can paint a face with such accuracy that you'd think you're looking at a photograph. But you'll never ever know those artists' names. Picasso didn't become Picasso by delivering accurate renderings of his subjects. An elbow here, a breast there — he had a distinct style that made him a star.

Would Vidal Sassoon have become a household name giving customers any old hairstyle they wanted?

> *You can have a car in any color you like, as long as it's black.*
>
> Henry Ford

They could get any haircut they wanted as long as it was the signature Sassoon cut.

If my client, the interior designer, wants to get known, she has to choose a path. She has to get off the fence and get known for something. She'll never become a star being the designer for everybody.

To Star or Not to Star? That is the Question

Stars know and accept that they aren't for everyone. A lounge singer singing cover tunes in a hotel lobby or a wedding dance band playing all the popular hits — they're unlikely to ever attract the spotlight regardless of how good they are. You gotta have a distinct style.

Elvis got noticed singing songs that had not been traditionally sung by a "white boy". The church-going, mama-loving "Elvis the Pelvis" couldn't keep his hips from gyrating on stage. When Ed Sullivan refused to film him from the waist down, Elvis drove the crowds wild, just by wiggling his little finger.

In the music industry, there's a category known as "sidemen", highly proficient professional musicians who play for various artists or as session musicians on the albums of the stars. They often have a more stable career than the stars themselves because they never really go out of fashion, but they rarely get the spotlight either.

Tribute Band or Tribute Bland?

I just dropped a vanload of kids at the local swimming pool and noticed that there was a concert in the park. "Elevation", a U2 tribute band was doing its best to wake up suburbia. Now, I don't know my U2 from my U3, but I do know one thing. If I'm going to stick around and fight off the mosquitoes, it's going to be for the genuine article, not for a Me2 tribute band. It's not that the musicians aren't as talented. They probably are. It's just that we want the real thing.

I'm still trying to get over the Dick Sergeant for Dick York switcheroo on *Bewitched* and that was eons ago.

Who wants to be a No-Name brand? Don't be easily replaceable. And don't be a Me2.

Stealing the Spotlight

Many people assume that the best role in a movie or play is the lead. I joked earlier about Robin never getting his own show, but often the sidekick, the character part, the best friend of the ingénue (the Rosie O'Donnell part), is the juiciest part, a part you can sink your teeth into and play with passion. Often, it's the part that'll get you noticed.

Remember the old TV show, *Happy Days*? Richie Cunningham played by Ron Howard was the lead role. But the actor that quickly emerged as the star was Henry Winkler, playing the role of "The Fonz", Arthur Fonzarelli. The Fonz started out as a bit part. But the character became so popular, he eventually became the show's focus. How did an actor with such a small role steal the spotlight and become the star? By adding definition, a black leather jacket over his original white T-shirt, a few trademark expressions, a girl on each arm (more on that below), an irresistible persona was created.

You don't have to be the industry leader to be a star. Good luck knocking Revlon or IBM off their thrones. But The Body Shop and Apple Computer took another approach. Each found a niche and carved out a great part for itself, what actors would call "a character part". These companies weren't trying to usurp the lead roles; they added color and definition to create memorable alternatives for their audience.

One of the best studies in character development on TV was *The Gilmore Girls*. Forget the main characters, Rory and her mom Lorelei. Check out the rest of the inhabitants of Stars Hollow — the crabby Mrs. Kim who runs the local antique shop, her repressed daughter Lane and the offbeat musician, Zack, whom Lane marries, Michel the snooty French concierge at the Inn, Sookie the chef, Emily the conservative pillar of society, Richard, her stuffed shirt husband, local gossips, Babette and Miss Patty, the odious media mogul Mitchum Huntzberger, Paris the sour-faced overachiever, Kirk the quirky... not sure what Kirk is, that's kinda his character. Each character is well defined and fascinating, each one a star in this truly ensemble cast. *Ugly Betty* makes another great case study.

Whenever I see 17 financial planners at a business meeting, I'm thinking "Guys, you really need to watch more TV." You wanna be seen in the marketplace? Develop your character. Add definition and color. Develop your brand. That's how you attract the spotlight.

When you attract the spotlight, you create your own stardom.

OK, so you've decided you want to be a star. Otherwise, you wouldn't still be reading. But what kind of star do you want to be?

When you attract the spotlight, you create your own stardom.

Getting Typecast

Every actor's first goal is just to get a part, any part. But once they've achieved a bit of success, most actors fear being "typecast", pigeonholed as only being able to play one type of character. Julie Andrews admits she spent years in therapy, partially as a result of her frustration at getting typecast in prissy, clean do-gooder type roles. I loved *The Sound of Music*. I've seen the movie 17 times. I had no idea that Julie resented being perceived as the prim and proper "whiter than snow" girl-guide characters she portrayed in *The Sound of Music* and *Mary Poppins*. Julie apparently has a bawdy sense of humor that she's rarely invited to display. I doubt Pamela Anderson gets many invitations to do Shakespeare.

As an entrepreneur, you generally want to get typecast. That's what branding is all about, the perception your audience, your customers and potential customers, have about you. But just like actors aren't always happy with the position they occupy in the minds of movie goers (Elvis longed to prove himself as a serious actor and cringed at having to sing silly songs in B movies), so businesses can be frustrated by their audience's perception of them.

Xerox makes photocopiers. They tried, without success, to sell us computers. Why didn't we buy computers from Xerox? Because they'd been typecast as manufacturers of photocopiers. It sometimes makes sense to "lay low", play a few bit parts, till you've decided what role you want to play in the market.

Evening at the Improv

Don't figure out your role on stage. In a play, no one sends actors on stage without assigning them each a particular character to play. And yet, many entrepreneurs are content to be improvisational actors. Improvisation is a great way to build your persona in the first place, but do it off Broadway.

If you want to get noticed in the marketplace, you have to define your character. Even improvisation troupes like Second City develop characters in improv and then repeat them and refine them till they enter their repertoire of well loved characters. A great place to workshop your character and develop your brand (and to practice the infomercials we'll work on in the next chapter) is the little local networking meeting. You'll build your confidence and hone your persona before you take it on the road.

But know, that if you don't cast yourself in a well defined role, you run the risk that the audience may cast you in a role you don't want. Or worse yet. You won't get cast at all.

POSITIONING

*R*emember the old movie stars who would only allow themselves to be filmed from one side? Their good side. "I'm ready for my close-up, Mr. DeMille."

Stars know how to position themselves. And not just physically.

To be a star, you don't have to be the best. You only have to be the best at positioning!

The theory of positioning, as explained by Trout and Ries, is that the mind contains slots, like drawers in a chest of drawers. Companies attempt to fill one of those drawers. Once a drawer is occupied, that "position" is taken. The role has been cast.

Dandruff Shampoo. Chances are that one product occupies that position in your mind. Getting rid of dandruff isn't the sexiest claim, but everyone knows what Head & Shoulders stands for. It's very difficult for another company to dislodge that thought and replace it with its own product.

So if the position you want is full, it may be easier to find yourself another drawer. In the toothpaste category, Crest already had the "no cavities" category, so Close Up grabbed "fresh breath".

Create Your Own Category

Or you can invent your own category. Rather than go head-to-head with the soda pop category leader, Coca-Cola, 7 UP created a new category, the "*Un*cola". If you're the only one in your category, chances are you'll be the best!

If you don't grab a position or create one, your audience may do your positioning for you, as it did with Julie Andrews.

What Are You Selling?

When I was 14 going on 15, I got to sing "I am 16 going on 17" in the coveted role of Liesl in *The Sound of Music*. It was an off off off Broadway production (Illinois), and I wasn't the only one who coveted the role. Instead of having understudies, the play was double cast, which meant that on the nights I wasn't playing Liesl, I was playing Sister Sophia and another actress, Terry, did the same. I guess they figured they could throw someone in at the last minute to play the nun and Terry and I could cover for each other as Liesl.

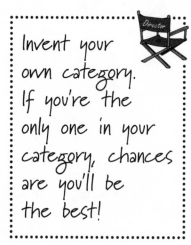

Invent your own category. If you're the only one in your category, chances are you'll be the best!

Double casting may make sense in theater, but it doesn't make sense in business.

Wearing Two Hats

Have you ever introduced yourself at a business function by saying "I'm here today wearing two hats." I hear that a lot. To your audience, that sounds like: "Hi, I'm a rocket scientist and I sell gift baskets on the side."

Don't be saying that! Choose one and wear it!

I know it's tempting. You think we'll be more impressed if we see the full range of your many talents. We won't.

The Power of Focus

Movie makers understand, better than anyone, the power of focus. Whatever you focus the camera lens on, that's what ends up on screen. Let's say you're videotaping a wedding. You could videotape the father of the bride getting drunk and knocking over the crystal centerpiece or you could capture the bride and groom having a quiet intimate moment. Same wedding, two entirely different pictures. You change the story you tell, the impact you have, the message you give, depending on what you focus on.

Choose one thing to focus on.

Some car companies do this really well. You know that old Jeep commercial where the guy stops at a gas station and asks for directions? The attendant tells him something like this, "The place you want is just over the mountain, so you have to go down here, turn right, left at the highway, around the bend…"

Meanwhile, the Jeep is halfway over the mountain. What's the message of that commercial? The message is "Jeep can go anywhere!"

"Hi, I'm a rocket scientist and I sell gift baskets on the side." Don't be saying that!

They don't mention that it has beautiful leather bucket seats or that it gets the best gas mileage. One message. You can go anywhere in a Jeep.

What does Volvo stand for? Safety. Everyone knows that. You never see a gorgeous model draped on the hood of a Volvo. (They tried to get me. I wasn't available.)

You Gotta Know What You're Selling

Mark McCormack, in *What They Don't Teach You at Harvard Business School*, tells a story of a guy running into his friend, Andre Heiniger, then chairman of Rolex, at a restaurant. The guy asks Heiniger, "How's the watch business?" Heiniger says, "I have no idea." The guy laughs, but Heiniger clarifies, "Rolex is not in the watch business. Rolex is in the luxury business."

You gotta know what you're selling!

It's no coincidence that many of the car companies put models on the hood of their cars. They know what they're selling — sex. And they don't need the models to do it.

The automobile is the most common sex symbol in our modern society.

> Jean Rosenbaum, M.D., *Is Your Volkswagen a Sex Symbol?*

The Ugly Brown Liquid

Let's say you're in the business of selling an ugly brown liquid. How do you do it? One company does it with paintings of gondolas in Venice, the gondolier enjoying a sensually shaped cup of coffee while he glides through the canal. What are they selling? Escape. Romance. Adventure. Sensuality.

45

It's still an ugly brown liquid! Another company sells it with a guy named Juan Valdez and a donkey. Another company sells a different ugly brown liquid, by getting Michael Jackson, Madonna, Britney Spears and Shakira to shake their assets on TV. They're selling youth, excitement, a new generation, since their main competitor already established itself first, over a hundred years ago, as the "real thing".

In many beer commercials you see young beautiful people dancing around at parties having the time of their lives. They're selling fun, a good time.

And so, the ugly brown liquids sell!

Roots

Roots throws a picture of a beaver on a sweatshirt and sells the romance of the Canadian wilderness, ironic since the Roots founders are two American boys from Detroit, Motor City, the farthest thing from the great outdoors that they're selling. They're also selling "Team Spirit" nostalgia with their university letter-style jackets. They're selling a sense of belonging. "Buy our jacket and you'll feel like part of the team." Not a bad idea in a country like Canada where isolation is a huge challenge. Roots was one of the first companies to package Canada and sell a Canadian lifestyle to the world.

Revlon

Charles Revson of Revlon said, "In our factories we sell perfume. In our stores we sell hope." And that's exactly what they're selling, the hope that you'll look like Cindy Crawford if you use their product. You won't. But that's the good thing about hope. It springs eternal, or so I read on a bumper sticker. Eternal enough to make cosmetics a multi-gazillion dollar business.

Quaker Oat, Campbell Soup

What are they selling? For years, these companies have consistently symbolized comfort, stability, nostalgia, an idealized childhood. That's how you create a strong brand.

Dove

Have you seen the Dove ads? A bunch of "real" women in underwear. Dove is trying to position itself as the champion of women's self esteem with its "Campaign for Real Beauty". Kinda makes you forget that UniLever, the company that makes Dove, also sells Slim Fast with women in bikinis.

Special K Cereal

Special K tried to appeal to women with a series of commercials depicting men in bars asking each other stereotypically female questions, "Does this make me look fat?" But these innovative commercials were eventually replaced by the Cindy Crawford type commercials when they didn't generate the sales they were expecting.

Harley Motorcycles

A new Harley Davidson dealership opened up in my neighborhood a few years ago and, I must admit, my first reaction was shock. What are bikers doing smack dab in the middle of suburbia? It only took a few minutes before it dawned on me. These guys know what they're selling. And to whom. They're selling "the rebel", freedom, "bad boy". You take some 53-year-old bald accountant with a beer belly, a wife, three kids and a mortgage, throw him on a Harley and all of a sudden, he's James Dean!

(I've been using this example in my speeches for some time and the other day I saw one of these guys outside of the bank. The seat on his bike looked like a Lazy Boy easy chair from the *That '70s Show* and the guy looked exactly as I've described him. I jokingly asked the guy "Where does the TV go?" and without missing a beat he said "I've been thinking about it.")

Marlboro
··············

I was explaining this concept to my daughter, Paloma, while we were out buying groceries. Kids always know what they're really buying. They know if they buy the right T-shirt they're buying "Cool".

I told her about a cigarette company, Philip Morris, who originally tried to sell Marlboros to women in the 20s with the tagline, "Mild as May". They even gave the cigarette a red filter tip so lipstick smudges wouldn't show. Didn't work. So they stuck a guy on a horse and made it the preferred brand of cowboys.

There's like 23 actual cowboys in the whole U.S.A., so how'd it become a leading brand? My guess is that an accountant or two snuck out and bought a pack. Marlboro knew what it was selling. What guy doesn't want to think of himself as a rugged Marlboro man?

Philip Morris eventually did connect with women, at least for a while. Remember, Virginia Slims? "You've got your own cigarette now, baby." I guess that got old after a while, but when I told my daughter about it, she immediately understood. "Oh, so they were selling feminism?" Smart kid.

Nike
·······

What are they selling? "Just Do It!" Empowerment.

And we pay money for this stuff! Big money!

Shoes for empowerment. Makeup for hope. Oatmeal for comfort. Coffee for escape.

We're not paying $200 for the shoes. We're paying because we believe that in those shoes we can "Go For It", in *those* shoes we can "Do It", in those shoes, we're invincible!

We've bought into the story. We're paying for how the story makes us feel!

Seth Godin, a must-read marketing writer, tells the story of a woman who was about to spend $125.00, a full day's salary, on a pair of limited edition Puma sneakers, sneakers that were made for three dollars in China.

> *She was imagining her dramatically improved life once other people saw how cool she was... The way Stephanie felt when she bought the Pumas was the product.*
>
> Seth Godin, *All Marketers Are Liars*

The Real Thing
····················

Entrepreneurs often don't know what they're really selling. Sometimes even the Big Boys get it wrong!

Coca-Cola, maybe you've heard of it. Granddaddy of colas. Along comes Pepsi, always in second place, and launches "The Pepsi Challenge". In blind taste tests, people said they liked Pepsi better, or so claimed Pepsi. Coke didn't believe them, so they conducted their own taste tests and much to their chagrin learned that Pepsi was telling the truth. People preferred the taste of Pepsi to Coke.

So Coke gets a brilliant idea! They sent their scientists back to the lab to come up with a new formula. Clearly they'd never heard of the expression "If it ain't broke, don't fix it", because fix it they did. They came up with a new formula and called this new drink (I'm wondering how many marketing gurus it took to come up with this name), "New Coke". Before launching this new product, they conducted more blind taste tests, and the results were very exciting. In blind taste tests, people said they preferred the taste of "New Coke" to Pepsi or Coke.

Well it's no big secret that New Coke bombed. It tanked. Big time. One of the biggest disasters in marketing history. New Coke only lasted seven weeks before they pulled it off the shelves. New Coke had to retreat with its tail between its legs. People wouldn't buy it. Why?

Maybe people weren't buying Coke for taste. Coke forgot that it was *The Real Thing*! The original.

In *The Other Guy Blinked*, Pepsi CEO, Roger Enrico, says "Coke was the American Dream in a bottle."

Yet, Coke temporarily lost sight of that. Coke allowed itself to be manipulated by Pepsi into making an incorrect assumption. Coke didn't have to play Pepsi's game. Coke was about tradition and the memories associated with it. Maybe Coke reminded a woman of that summer on the beach when the blonde surfer boy kissed her. Or of Christmas time. Why else do we collect the old glass bottles or the memorabilia trays?

I recently snuck out of an Internet marketing seminar to visit the Coca-Cola Museum in Atlanta, Georgia — a marketer's paradise. They screened a bunch of old Coke commercials reminding the world that "Things go better with Coke", a campaign that emphasized Coke's intention to be our companion for life. And it wasn't just hype. During World War II, Coke took a financial risk setting up portable bottling plants just so soldiers on the front lines could get a taste of home in a glass.

> *See that every man in uniform gets a bottle of Coca-Cola for 5 cents wherever he is and whatever the cost to the company.*
> Robert Woodruff, Then President of Coca-Cola

It was genius of Pepsi to change the dialog to one of taste because it couldn't compete with Coke in the tradition department. Coke would have been better not to play along.

Coke quickly came to its senses and made a strong recovery, renaming the original formula "Coke Classic", thus responding to customers' outcries, refocusing on tradition and reconnecting with the fans. But it's a great lesson for any entrepreneur.

If you make up the game, i.e., create a category that you're most suited to winning, it's a no-brainer that you're more likely to *win* that game. Best taste? Pepsi. *Un*cola? 7 UP. Classic? Coke. There's no shortage of categories. The only limits are our creativity and our ability to entice the audience to what we've created.

Put On Your Own Show
••••••••••••••••••••••••••••••

Stars never put themselves at the mercy of other people's games. I have a client who came to me to coach her for a public speaking contest. I told her that, as confident as I am in my abilities as a speaker and as a singer, and even having won talent contests in the past, I would never again put myself in that position.

Why stand side by side with other people who are trying to show that they are better than you? I overheard a guy who sells high-end televisions telling someone that there was a reason that a particular leading TV brand (rhymes with "pony"; I'm not the one who said it) never allows itself to be displayed side by side with its competitors. He claimed that by having its own little niche within the store, this brand avoids being shown up by the competition. If it's true, they're smart.

Stars set up their own stage and put on their own show, one where the lighting and sound and audience and time of the year and time of day and everything else best suits them and their talents.

Predictably, the contest did not go as well as my client had hoped, largely, in my opinion, because of her lack of control over the circumstances.

After Coke's recovery with Coke Classic, the tradition drawer was clearly taken, so Pepsi made a play for the "youth drawer". And the "Pepsi Generation" was born. Pepsi became the drink not only for young people but for the young at heart, the aging boomers with fat wallets who want to recapture their youth by drinking a youthful drink.

Ask Yourself. What Are You Really Selling?
....

You're an insurance salesperson. You rank up there in popularity somewhere between dentists and income tax auditors. But you can change all that. It's not about the benefits of term insurance versus whole life or statistics on the frequency of scary diseases. It's about peace of mind. A sense of security, that whatever happens, you'll be OK. You don't have to remind us about the scary things to get us to buy. Freedom 55 had it right. Youthful grey haired people walking hand in hand on the beach. Where do I sign?

If you insist on scaring your prospects (most marketers will tell you that customers will pay more to avoid pain than seek pleasure), then at least be clever about it. Altamira Investment Services has a brilliant print campaign featuring a granny wearing a Walmart type smock, "Have A Great Day" button and all, reminding us of our fate if we don't prepare for retirement.

Are You Selling a Truffle or a Hershey Bar?

I don't have grey hair yet, but if I did, I'd be wanting to walk along that beach with some Heather Locklear hair. L'Oréal was brilliant when it came to promoting it's hair color product, Preference. "It costs a little more, but I'm worth it." If women chose anything other than Preference, they were telling themselves they weren't worth enough to buy the good stuff.

In *Don't Go Shopping for Hair Care Products Without Me*, author Paula Begoun tells of a study in which 100 women were given two identical conditioners but told that one was a very expensive salon product while the other was an inexpensive drugstore conditioner. A full 80% of the women who tried both reported that the "expensive" conditioner performed better!

Psychology professor and author, Dr. Robert Cialdini (*Influence: Science and Practice*) tells a story about a friend who ran a Native American jewelry store in Arizona. His friend was having trouble selling her turquoise pieces and decided to just unload them, so she left a quick note for her employee telling her "All Jewelry × ½". The employee misread the note and doubled the price of everything. By the time the owner returned, all the jewelry had sold.

Lest you think it's just women who fall for this stuff, let me tell you about another study. In *Remote Control*,

Frank Mankiewicz and Joel Swerdlow report an experiment conducted over 30 years ago at the Wharton School at the University of Pennsylvania.

Two hundred and fifty beer lovers were grouped by personality type and given four different brands of beer to taste. Each of the brands was given a different "connotation free" name (Bix, Zim, Waz or Biv). The beer drinkers were shown story boards of proposed television commercials, each designed to appeal to one of the four personality types.

After seeing the story boards, the subjects were given the various beers to drink and asked to comment. Not only did each of them claim to taste the difference between them, several chose one as their favorite and "many said that one brand or another was not 'fit for human consumption'." The punchline? No big surprise here. All the beer was identical, taken from one brew, from the same vat.

> Once you have the right what, the how is easy. How can you sell it, if you don't know what it is?

What makes this even more interesting is that the subjects chose their favorite beer as predicted by their personality types and influenced by the proposed commercials.

It's not about the ugly brown liquid. You gotta know what you're really selling.

Once you have the right *what*, the *how* is easy. How can you sell it, if you don't know what it is?

WHO'S YOUR AUDIENCE?

A shoe factory sends two marketing scouts to a region of Africa to study the prospects for expanding business. One sends back a telegram saying,

SITUATION HOPELESS STOP NO ONE WEARS SHOES

The other writes back triumphantly,

GLORIOUS BUSINESS OPPORTUNITY STOP THEY HAVE NO SHOES

Rosamund and Benjamin Zander, *The Art of Possibility*

Who's Your Audience?
....

*Y*ou can't go two seconds as an entrepreneur without someone asking you "Who's your target market?" It's not always obvious.

Don't worry if you aren't sure who your audience is yet. Just be observant and watch for trends.

I heard a guy, recently, tell a story about how he put on seminars to teach couples how to accumulate wealth. He got a small, but respectable, showing. One night, a woman came up to him and thanked him for really speaking to women. As a result of her comment, he went out on a limb and billed the next seminar as a *women's* wealth building seminar. He got a record 800 participants! His average audience grew to about 1000 women a shot. He found his audience, or more accurately, his audience found him.

Be On Reception

The book, *Compact Classics*, had only sold a small number of copies when someone commented to the author that

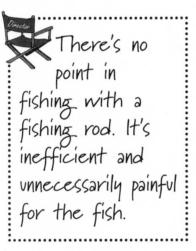

There's no point in fishing with a fishing rod. It's inefficient and unnecessarily painful for the fish.

he loved the book because each story was short enough to read in the bathroom. Fortunately, the author was paying attention and repackaged the classics compilation as *The Great American Bathroom Book* with the subtitle *Single-Sitting Summaries of All-Time Great Books*.

Based on observation, rather than targeting, *Compact Classics* was able to reposition its product from a textbook-style compilation to a popular phenomenon. The book quickly went from obscurity to best seller, selling a million and a half copies and counting.

When I started my coaching practice, I promoted myself as a publicity coach. But many of the people who ended up becoming my audience were more interested in learning how to present in public and stand out, how to add humor and get noticed.

I thought my audience would be mostly entrepreneurs who are just starting a business. I do get a few, but many of my clients are well established in business, several have been named "Entrepreneur of the Year". It also never occurred to me that many of my clients would be professional speakers and trainers and even radio and TV show hosts. My audience found me.

Forget the Fishing Rod. Use a Net

Entrepreneurs waste a lot of time chasing "leads". Many networking groups promote the "lead chasing" concept. My view? There's no point in fishing with a fishing rod. It's inefficient and unnecessarily painful for the fish.

I prefer to just lay out an enticing net and see who chooses to swim in. When I introduce myself to an audience of 80 people at a business event, the four or five people who come up to me afterwards are never the ones I would have "targeted".

So, don't worry, yet, about finding your audience. We're going to do some more character development first.

Your job is to become visible and stay visible. Your job is to keep the lamp burning, like at a lighthouse, so your audience can find you.

> Your job is to keep the lamp burning, like at a lighthouse, so your audience can find you.

CHARACTER DEVELOPMENT: DEVELOPING THE PERSONA, CREATING THE BRAND

"'Cause You've Got — Personality!"

In order to be visible through the chaos and clutter nowadays, you gotta stand out. You already know that. You gotta have a rich distinct persona and you gotta show it. You've chosen your role. Now, like in a play, we have to flesh out the character so it'll be memorable.

"What's My Motivation?"

During the character development process, actors are always asking their directors "What's my motivation?"

And the standard theater joke answer is "To get paid."

In business, this is absolutely the real answer. Your motivation to breathe life into your character and deliver a stellar performance is just that — "to get paid".

Take a Stand
....

What do you stand for? Your audience will want to know. If you want to get noticed, you gotta stand for something.

Don't Give 'Em Too Many Choices
....

"And the sign said long-haired freaky people need not apply." Remember the 1971 song, "Signs", by the Five Man Electrical Band? Originally released as a B-side recording and going nowhere fast, the record is a perfect illustration of the "Don't Give 'Em Too Many Choices" principle.

> ...we had been trained to think about what it takes to make a radio hit, and that song wasn't it. Finally we changed record labels [and] reissued the record with "Signs" on both sides, so disc jockeys couldn't play the wrong one by accident.
> Les Emmerson, quoted by Liisa Ladouceur,
> *Words & Music*

They wanted a hit. So they only gave 'em one choice. The result? A hit! The lesson? Don't give 'em too many choices. They may not pick you, but at least they'll know where you stand. Am I right or am I right?

Do you remember McDonald's pizza? If you were in the mood for pizza, tell me, is McDonald's the place you'd choose to go? They've tried fajitas, wraps and even serve bratwurst and lobster in some locations. Why is the company always the last to know? The audience knows. McDonald's means hamburgers.

What's a Chevrolet? A large, small, cheap, expensive car... or truck.
Al and Laura Ries, *22 Immutable Laws of Branding*

Saturn got it right, at least till GM started back-seat driving, by developing a warm and sympathetic corporate personality that removed the "yuck factor" from women's car buying experiences. Saturn aired commercials showing sympathetic car salesmen picking up customers at the airport, understanding when a customer had to cancel an order because of a job loss and delivering a car with a gift of a car seat already in it to a pregnant customer. They even went the extra mile by holding Saturn Homecoming events, drawing tens of thousands of Saturn owners to make the trek to the Spring Hill, Tennessee plant to commune with the mechanics who made their cars. There's even a fan club.

Create Your Own Community

Deadheads, Fredheads, Fruheads. These are fans of musicians The Grateful Dead, Fred Eaglesmith and Moxy Fruvous respectively.

Saturn owners are (or maybe were) a community. Harley owners are a community. What you're going for are "sleep overnight on the sidewalk to get concert tickets" type evangelists. This creates energy around your brand and reinforces your persona. More on this in Chapter 5.

The Open Road

Harley Davidson has developed a rich vibrant company persona — a brilliant example of this principle at work. Check out their website. Harley holds events all over the world and their mantra is "Owning a Harley Davidson Motorcycle isn't about having. It's about doing. Experiencing the world in every sense." A word of caution if you go to their site. It's got me seriously thinking of trading in my 7-seater kidmobile and taking to the open road!

(Author Note: When I finally got a live body at their corporate head office, I was told that 1200 people worked there and got thrown into voice mail hell. Kinda killed the whole open road thing for me. Made me want to write them a whole new mantra "It's not about doing. It's about waiting." Definitely colored the persona. On the other hand, maybe all 1200 of them are out riding...)

The Body Shop, Apple Computers, L'Oréal, Ben and Jerry's, Smucker's Jam — each has cultivated a unique personality based on the background of its owner or its customers or the story of how the company came into being. And the persona is enhanced by including the customers and employees in the experience. Walmart uses photos of employees and their kids in its weekly flyers. Each of these companies has carved out a niche with a loyal following.

Eat the Red Ones Last — Create a Brand Ritual
••

Tell me, when you eat your Smarties, do you eat the red ones last?

How 'bout Oreos? How do you eat your Oreo cookies? 97% of the respondents to a nationwide survey knew exactly how they eat their Oreos. They knew whether they were "dunkers", "twisters" or "biters". (Dunkers are the "most popular and best looking at any gathering" according to the press release at the Kraft Newsroom.)

Martin Lindstrom, author of *BRANDsense*, encourages companies to create brand-based rituals and to engage customers with other senses beyond sight and sound, senses like smell, touch and taste. The 3 P.M. Snicker's break at work. Makes sense. Great way to add flavor and color to your company's character and get buy-in.

Start a Movement

Why stop with rituals? Create a whole movement! Great way to attract. People love controversy. They love a cause. They love to jump on board. Flower Power in the 60s. (Bet someone made a killing on flowers...) Women's lib in the 70s. Nancy Reagan's "Just Say No" anti-drug campaign in the 80s. The low carb thing. Atkins. Dove's "Campaign For Real Beauty". If you start the movement, you can be at the forefront of that movement. Not a bad place for a star.

It's scary how powerful this technique is. Sadly, it's used as often for evil as it is for good. But if you can harness this power for a worthwhile cause, you'll be amazed at the results.

If you'd come up with a natural lawn care product years ago, you could have been at the forefront of an anti-pesticide movement. Activist, Anita Roddick, used a similar strategy to build The Body Shop to where it is today, committing to social and environmental change. What a Dame. (No really. She was.) It doesn't even have to be your idea. You just have to be the one to "take it public".

Starting a movement doesn't have to be big or political. It's not the subject of the movement that makes it work, but rather the passion and energy behind it.

Don't be standing on a street corner with a clip board or petition. That's for bit players. Write a manifesto. Make a movie. (Worked for *The Secret*.) Have a credo, a mantra. The more outrageous it is, the more chance it'll work, the more you'll stand out from the crowd. We're not talking corporate mission statement here.

Get some publicity for your movement. (See Chapter 5.) And have stuff. Your "stuff" will become a symbol of the ideals behind that movement. (Reminds me of the sandal in Monty Python's *Life of Brian*...) Your symbol can become a potential source of income. But don't make the mistake of cashing in your chips too soon. The followers in your movement will be more valuable to you down the line if you don't try to sell to them yet. Just focus on building the following, building momentum, building the fan base. If you continue to build it, eventually people will beg you to sell to them because they'll want some of what you've got.

> ...*few stronger emotions exist than the need to belong and make meaning.*
> Douglas Atkin, *The Culting of Brands*

I'm not just talkin' the "Pepsi Generation" here. A movement goes a step further. If you give people a place to belong, a place to feel like they matter, like they're making a difference, you'll build your platform. Eventually they'll not only ask to buy stuff from you, they'll actually volunteer to help you distribute it to others.

So how do you apply this to your business? Here's a perfect example. I remember, when I was a kid, getting a little red "I Am Loved" button at the Peoples Jewellers store in the local shopping center. Funny how all these years later, I still remember not only what the little red button looked like, but also the store where I got it. I thought it was a Peoples Jewellers promotion, but, on researching it, I found out that it was a movement that started about 40 years ago in Kansas City. Barnett Helzberg

Jr., of Helzberg Diamonds, had just had his marriage proposal accepted. The guy was ecstatic. He was loved and wanted the world to know it. So he produced these little red buttons with the words, "I Am Loved", printed in white. The idea spread like wildfire, buttons were given to presidents, celebrities and soldiers in Vietnam. 44 million buttons later, you can still order yourself a button in any of 9 languages. The buttons were, and still are, free, but they did put Helzberg Diamonds on the map.

"Talkin' 'Bout a Revolution"?

If you've really accessed your inner *chutzpah*, you may be thinking, why stop at a movement? How 'bout a revolution? Tempting. And it worked for one Canadian politician whose "Common Sense Revolution" got him the title of Premier of his province.

Proceed with caution. This can be tricky. While it has to be over the top to succeed, you gotta go in remembering the old expression "the bigger they are, the harder they fall". When the revolution is over, you don't know who'll still be standing. I'd recommend building it a little slower, organically. Build a really solid base of support. Grass roots. If you don't want to be the flavor of the month, stick with a movement.

You're Nobody Till Somebody Hates You

The reason the little red buttons worked so well is that we all want to know that we are loved, but I always tell my clients that they'll know they've succeeded in crafting a clear enough persona when somebody takes shots at them. You're nobody till somebody hates you. The Body Shop, Saturn, Walmart, even America's sweetheart, Oprah, they all have critics, vocal critics. More on critics in Chapter 6, but for now, it's enough to know that if you have critics, you must be doing something right! If the Pope or the police haven't condemned Madonna's act recently, she knows she's losing her touch.

People and companies that sit on the fence generally don't have critics. There's nothing distinct enough about them to criticize. The sad truth is that they probably aren't even being noticed at all.

Let It All Hang Out — Almost!

Stars aren't afraid to let it all hang out. Look at all the extra points Oprah scored with her audience by letting us in, probably the first prominent TV personality to openly discuss her battle with her weight. We only loved her more for it.

> If the Pope or the police haven't condemned Madonna's act recently, she knows she's losing her touch.

This is a woman who understands drama. Who else would drag a little red wagon containing 67 lbs of chicken fat, representing the weight she lost, onto the stage?

But notice also, that it's often a well orchestrated "let it all hang out". A star will reveal just enough to create the bond, and to keep us hooked, without destroying the illusion that makes her a star. A star is always a bit bigger than life.

Behind the Scenes
....

Years ago, I was in a night club in Havana, Cuba (I'm not talking Tropicana; it was candle lit and intimate) and I was captivated by a wonderful torch singer sequined from head to toe. After the show, I went up to her and asked if I could get the music to one of her songs, so I could perform it myself. She invited me to come to her apartment the next day.

To say that the apartment was a "hole in the ground" would be inaccurate, because it was on the sixth floor of a dilapidated building without a functioning elevator. The walls in the one bedroom apartment she shared with six others hadn't seen paint in 20 years. She appeared in an outfit that made the walls look fresh. I remember this visit clearly because it was the first time in my life that I had seen such a striking difference between appearance and reality. And yet, when she was on stage in that night club, the reality was that she's a star. She was bigger than life.

Few of us can live our lives in sequins, nor would we want to. It's important to find a way to be a star that's close enough to our reality that we can actually live it.

Comedian, Josh Blue, found a way to incorporate his cerebral palsy into his routine and walked away with the title "Last Comic Standing" in the celebrated TV competition. What was he going to do — pretend he didn't have it? Gordon Paynter, a blind standup comic, opened shows with "Well, you smell like a good audience!"

Avis was an unprofitable company until they let it all hang out. They weren't the leaders. So why should people buy from them? Because "We Try Harder".

Your persona has to be rooted in authenticity or it won't work.

The Casting Couch
························

Whatever you do, choose the rest of your cast wisely. Whether you're part of an ensemble cast, or an entrepreneurial one-man show, you get to determine who your co-stars are. You choose whom you do business with, whom you hang out with.

Any self help guru, from Tony Robbins on down, will tell you that whom you hang out with can affect your success, hugely. Would *Seinfeld* have been the huge hit it was without Elaine, George and Kramer? It's the "Charlie's Angels Effect": Three Pretty Heads are Better Than One. The TV show, *Friends,* was a hit because all six main characters and the actors who played them, relative unknowns at the beginning, had star quality. Hang out with stars and you will shine.

"You Oughta Be in Pictures"
·····································

One of my clients is an old bag. Not my description, hers. She runs a hot lunch programme for schools and when she came to me a few years ago, she was hiding behind "the lunch bag", a little character she had created. The company persona was good but we made it even stronger by sticking her in a red gingham apron and sending her into the spotlight to network with "the suits". We cut up her corporate brochure and threw some "1950s mom baking apple pie" images into it. The result? She won entrepreneur of the year, got national media coverage and now has franchises across the country.

"Let Them Eat Bread!"

One company that wasn't content to sit on the shelf like a loaf of white bread was Levy's Rye Bread which was marketed with a poster showing an adorable Japanese kid obviously enjoying a Levy's Rye Bread sandwich. The tagline read "You Don't Have to be Jewish to Love Levy's Real Jewish Rye". Others in the poster series included a typical Irish cop, a Native American, an Italian mama. The 1949 campaign, which set Manhattan on fire, was so memorable it's still being talked about today — and the posters sell for big bucks.

You are the picture. You. Your business. What you wear, what your store or office looks like, that's the frame. Frame yourself well!

THE WARDROBE DEPARTMENT

Making an Entrance

••••••••••••••••••••••••••

*Y*ou don't have to burst into the courtroom with an oversized hat shading your face like Joan Collins in the 80s hit, *Dynasty*, or like Vanessa Williams, almost 30 years later, in *Ugly Betty*, to make an impression, but there is something to be said for making an entrance. Sometimes, it's not enough to just let your natural color shine through. You have to kick it up a notch, not so much exaggerate as to accentuate!

It's like makeup. Makeup shouldn't mask; it should enhance and complement your natural beauty. I don't wear makeup except on stage, as most actors do to accentuate their features so they can be seen from a distance.

At business functions, you're often meeting people for the first time. If you kick it up a notch (not too much, or it's fake), what's unique and attractive about you will be easily visible in an already processed and digestible form.

Showcasing
....

Most actors' unions put on annual showcases, productions put on specifically for the purpose of showing off the actors to their best advantage.

Stars know how to showcase themselves. What's showcasing? A diamond doesn't look like much when they find it in the mines of South Africa. A diamond needs to be cut, shaped, presented and showcased, like at Tiffany, on black velvet, in 14-karat gold claws as a solitaire ring.

My second oldest daughter, the one I affectionately call "Daughter Number Two", has been a spectacular chef since she first made a cake by herself at the age of seven. She's always making these amazing concoctions and my job is to scout out and buy her fantastic colorful original "presentation plates", plates that will showcase her latest creation.

How you look, how you showcase yourself, is key. I'm not talking about whether your nail polish matches your lipstick or whether you wear white after Labor Day. But graphic designers shouldn't look like accountants. Even accountants shouldn't look like accountants.

Professional doesn't mean boring!

After one of my seminars, I got two comment cards that said that they loved the way I was dressed! It was summer and I was wearing a casual Carribean blue print top, white capri pants and sandals. They said it made them feel comfortable that I was approachable.

Apparently, the week before, some fancy shmancy image consultant told them they should wear suits to seminars. And especially if they were ever giving a seminar, they should wear a well tailored suit.

Says who?

Stars Break the Rules

In fact, stars make up the rules! Don't become a clone.

Kick Up Your Heels

Centuries ago, men wore high heeled shoes (before women ever did) and were ornately dressed. By the late nineteenth century, men adopted a drab uniform called a "suit". Less than 50 years later, business-

Stars break the rules. In fact, they make up the rules!

women followed and we became a nation of "suit people", as indistinguishable as penguins.

"Dress for Success"?

What you wear *does* matter. Hugely. But personally, I cringe whenever I hear the expression "Dress for Success". It's usually the title of some archaic book or seminar dictating appropriate skirt lengths and sharing shoulder pad tips. We don't need any more "cufflinks must match the tie-clip" advice.

I approach the issue of wardrobe from an actor's point of view. What should I wear to communicate more about my character, to make my role more visible and consistent. How would I dress this character?

You have to dress to communicate the image you're trying to sell. And the roots of that image have to be authentic. Your audience will notice inconsistencies, if there are any, in what you say, how you say it and how you look, whether in person, on paper or at your premises. Anything that doesn't add up will make your prospective client uneasy, suspicious possibly, even though he may not be aware of the source of his discomfort.

I met a woman, a few months ago, whom I thought was the person who hired me to give the speech that evening. We'd only spoken on the phone, but upon just seeing her, before the woman even opened her mouth, I said "You're not Liz!"

I had formed a whole image in my mind of the woman over the phone based on her phone voice, her mannerisms and her level of confidence. Turns out, I was right. The woman I was being introduced to was her co-worker, Brenda, who was much more outgoing. I had sized her up in just seconds from her look and her body language, before she even opened her mouth. *Blink* indeed.

Dress for the Part

In the old TV westerns, the bad guy wore black. The good guy wore white. The saloon floozy wore red. You knew who they were. The "girl next door" would stick to paisley or pastels. She wouldn't dream of wearing red, any more than the good guy would wear black.

The Man in Black

Although not a bad guy, Johnny Cash went out of his way to remind us that he was no choirboy either, by consistently wearing black, boots and all. He claimed that, in the beginning, he and his band wore black because that was the only color they had that matched, but eventually his long black jackets became his trademark.

He even cemented his "I've been around" image, when, in spite of the skepticism of his record company, he recorded an album *Johnny Cash at Folsom Prison*, live in a penitentiary with an audience of inmates. The result? A hugely successful album and a hugely successful career.

The Clothes of Camelot

Like Audrey Hepburn, Jacqueline Kennedy (later Jackie O) was a master at using wardrobe to create her own personal brand, inspiring a slew of books to be written about her, including *The Clothes of Camelot* and *Jackie Style*.

The book about *my* personal clothing style hasn't yet hit the stands, but I'll confide in you that I never felt comfortable in the corporate wool (or polyester) three-piece-suit wearing world or in the robes I had to wear to court as a barrister. I am myself in 100% cotton, sandals and no makeup. During my "Lawyer Barbie" years, I tore off the pantyhose the second I walked in the door.

You gotta observe yourself and be honest. You gotta know what's comfortable and real for you and what isn't. That said, if what's comfortable for you is "soccer mom chic", there ain't nothing wrong with accenting that for extra definition. Would we recognize Willie Nelson without his braids?

Paper Wardrobe

No, I'm not talking about those little paper dresses kids used to fold into paper dolls. But how you look does apply to your printed portfolio as well, your business cards and other paper stuff. Make sure they're not boring.

If you're a real estate agent, don't stick your picture (you know the one taken 19 years ago) on the left side of your card like everyone else. I was driving recently beside a real estate agent who had a huge photo on the side of her car — blonde, all teeth, beautiful. Saw the driver and thought to myself, "How nice. She let her grandma borrow the car." Stopped at red light and realized it was her! Who are we fooling here?

By the way, if you're not a real estate agent, don't stick your photo on the left side of your card. Why? We might think you're a real estate agent!

Business cards cost peanuts nowadays. Keep revising till they're "Out of the Ballpark" fabulous!

Should you put a photo on your business card? Some say it creates a feeling of familiarity and trust. Singers and authors are told that, if they're not famous, putting their face on the cover of a book or CD screams amateur. I'd say, stay away from your mug on your card unless your look is a major part of your business' persona.

Less is More
••••••••••••••••

Cards are puny. This is prime real estate. Some cards are so busy with information (logos, business descriptions, lists of services, testimonials and 337 ways to make contact) that they look like a jumble of words. Nothing stands out and the message is diluted. Remember, every word is competing with every other word for attention.

I devote 90% of my card to a colorful image and the rest to my name and telephone number and web site. When people receive my card, they often comment, "It's colorful, like you". Ya Man!

Do It by the Book
••••••••••••••••••••••

You want the ultimate folding business card? Create a 200-page business card — a book. You've heard the expression "My book is my calling card". Instant recognition.

Instant expert status. Someone might even pay you for one. Nothing to sneeze at.

A Canadian stock broker did just that. He put his thoughts on paper, self-published a book from the basement of his house and next thing you know, David Chilton became not only a recognized expert on financial planning, but a best-selling author to boot.

Don't Get Fleeced

I heard a marketing type speaking recently about a financial planner who came to her to develop printed material for a large women's trade show. The client got stuck competing for attention not only with 30 other financial planners but also with vendors of sex toys and bra fitting specialists. To make matters worse, this financial planner specialized in divorce, not a pleasant topic at the best of times.

The marketing company came up with an innovative concept: "Getting Divorced? Don't Get Fleeced", which they punctuated with pictures of sheep all over the brochures and posters. The sheep were labeled "House", "Pension", "Alimony". They managed to find the biggest concern of divorcing women and attach an unforgettable visual to it. This financial planner is now known as the "Sheep Lady" and she is remembered.

But One Ma'am's Lamb is Another Man's Ham

You know how in Hollywood, most serious actors won't even consider a nude scene unless it really has to do with the story? If you are going to use a visual to add color, make sure it relates to the message you're trying to communicate.

The Lamest Lamb — "Ba-a-a-a-ad" Visuals

I keep seeing billboards and bench advertising for a local real estate agent whose last name is "Lamb". His ads feature a lamb's body attached to the agent's head, surrounded by other farm animals. If you ask me, these ads make him look more like another barnyard animal.

He may argue that, at least, I remember his name. It's true. He did get noticed, "lampshade on the head at parties" noticed. It's not going to make me hire him to sell my house.

In one episode of *The Apprentice*, a spirited East Indian candidate was accused of not being a team player because she refused to wear a silly costume. Trump pointed out that even he dressed up as a chicken on *Saturday Night Live*. But I think Trump missed a distinction. Once your reputation is solid, it's good to show that you don't take yourself too seriously. But someone who's trying to establish her credibility at the outset might want to think twice before putting on a donkey suit.

The Blue Box

The lamb guy could learn a thing or two from the keepers of the box. Tiffany understands showbiz. From their sparkly product to their Tiffany Blue Boxes, Tiffany focuses on eliciting an emotional response from its audience. Do they succeed? Ya, Man. The color of the box hasn't changed since it was introduced in 1837 and the box itself has become a symbol of style and sophistication.

As early as 1906, the *New York Sun* reported:

Tiffany has one thing in stock that you cannot buy of him for as much money as you may offer; he will only

*give it to you. And that is one of his boxes. The rule
of the establishment is ironclad, never to allow a box
bearing the name of the firm, to be taken out of the
building except with an article which has been sold by
them and for which they are responsible.*

Would the box have outlived Tiffany himself if he kept
changing the color of the box from season to season, or
if he had diluted his message? Unlikely.

*Tiffany wants you to forget the product and remember
where it came from.*
  Denise Meyer (Quoted by Stephanie Blackburn in
                 Tiffany & Company, A Case Study)

WHAT'S IN A NAME?

A lot! A name can change your life.

My youngest daughter, Aviva, once did a speech on names for school and she uncovered two interesting experiments. The first had to do with how intelligent a name sounds. Eighty teachers were each given eight essays to mark, all about the same quality. They put four popular names on half of them and they put four unusual names on the others. The marks were revealing. Hubert got a grade lower than Michael. Bertha got a grade and a half lower than Lisa. With one teacher, Adele received the highest mark. The teacher later admitted that Adele sounded like an intelligent name.

The second experiment was conducted to determine whether a name had to do with the person's popularity. The results? No surprise to anyone named Gertrude or Harriet. The people with more popular names were better liked.

Me, I'll take interesting over popular any day, although I must admit, I didn't feel that way as a kid. If you have an interesting name, embrace it!

When I first started singing professionally, an industry heavyweight suggested that "Tsufit" was too unusual for

North American audiences and that I should change it. To what? Debbie? Cindy? People remember me.

I heard Oprah once say that when she was starting out, she was told by the TV station hanchos that she should change her name to Suzy. And now — *The Suzy Winfrey Show!*

Hurray for Hollywood!

In the tradition of Rock Hudson and Cary Grant, Leonardo DiCaprio was told to change his name to "Lenny Williams". (Sounds a little "lounge-singer-in-a-skintight-leopard-skin-body-suit"-ish to me.) Ramon Estevez became famous under the name Martin Sheen. But his sons, Charlie Sheen and Emilio Estevez, both seem to be doing equally well despite their name choices. How 'bout Orville Redenbacher? Would Ken Smith Popcorn sell as well?

It's not just Hollywood types that shed their names. Anthony J. Mahavorick did OK for himself under his new name. (*Clue*: He's mentioned elsewhere in this book.)

I was planning to use Orville Redenbacher as an example of how an ordinary guy succeeded with an ordinary name. Well, the joke's on me. Turns out Orville's real name is Sam Henry. I guess there *is* such a thing as too ordinary.

The Business Name

If you're thinking of naming your business John Smith and Associates, think again. An inspired business name can change your life.

When Kaile Warren was no longer able to run his small construction business after a debilitating car accident, he fell into debt, lost his wife and his car and eventually found himself homeless. The guy prayed for a break and it came in the form of a name. Rent a Husband® is now a successful franchised handyman business and Warren is an author, speaker and a regular home improvement correspondent for *The Early Show* on **CBS**. He's even trademarked the tagline "Tall, Dark and Handy."

Many debut CDs are named simply after the artist. When I made my CD, it occurred to me that having a name for my CD would give me "two kicks at the can" instead of one. People might buy it because they'd heard of me or because the title attracted them.

But, when I started my coaching practice, I strongly resisted using a business name at all. I figured they'd be coming for coaching with me, Tsufit, so why did I need another name? A lot of consultants and coaches feel that way.

I was sitting in on a business course around that time, and they made us come up with a name anyway. Just to shut them up, I threw out "Follow That Dream!" I ended up keeping it. It's true most people come for me, but people who don't know me are attracted by the name. It's crucial you think like a star when you name your business!

Don't even think of naming your business LPA Financial or JWD Interiors. Initials are boring and no one can remember them! IBM and KFC didn't start out that way.

Making Your Name the Star Attraction

A consumer complaint handling business could have been called "Consumer Complaint Consulting Services" or any number of similarly drab names. Instead, the inspired owner named it "Rent-a-Kvetch", a name which landed her interviews on *Oprah*, *The Today Show* and *Good Morning America*. Though she "retired from professional kvetching" years ago, New York native B.L. Ochman says she still gets regular interview requests.

Some Names Are Just Garbage

Brian Scudamore launched a multi-million dollar business without even a high school diploma. He had something better. He had an incredible understanding of the difference between a bit player and a star.

Scudamore tells the story of being in the McDonald's Drive Through and noticing a truck hauling garbage that said "Mark's Hauling" on it. Scudamore realized that Mark was never going to be a star. It occurred to him that no one had ever professionally branded junk removal. So he decided to become the "'Fed Ex' of junk removal."

His first attempt at naming his company was "The Rubbish Boys", not bad, sounds like a movie title, but he eventually changed it because "rubbish" isn't a common word in North America and because eventually many of his employees were women.

So he renamed it "1-800-Got-Junk" (relentlessly pestering the government department that owned the toll free number to sell him the rights) and quickly attained blockbuster status. Pizza Pizza had, many years ago, created a brilliant marketing campaign by setting its phone number 967-1111 to music. Scudamore upstaged them by making the phone number the business name.

Who do you think gets more calls? "Excellent Computer Consulting Services" or "Nerds on Site"? A fabulous business name is often far more valuable than the bricks and mortar of the company it represents.

Speaking of names, I was thinking the other day, why aren't there any Jewish car companies? We could sell cars. We'd do it differently though. You know how all the regular car companies name their cars after horses? Pinto, Pony, Colt, Bronco, Mustang. You know what we'd name them after? Food! The Toyota Kugel. The Chrysler Knish. The Dodge Danish. The Honda Herring. And for Passover, the Mazda Matza — special edition. And we wouldn't be sticking some leggy blonde model on the hood of the car. You know what we'd put? A jar of pickles. Some Polskie Orgorkies would sell that car!

Name Your Stuff
·····················

Don't just name yourself and your business. Name your stuff — every product and service in your business should have a name. It's fun and it sells.

I had always sold my coaching services in sessions, based on units of time. I recently decided to start naming some of my services and now offer little mini "Speak Critiques" for entrepreneurs wanting feedback on their networking introductions. It's like the bite-sized Mars Bars on the counter at the drug store. You buy one and soon, you're lugging home cases of Mars Bars. Maybe that's just me...

Make sure you get the name right.

If you're selling a new kind of carbonated sugar water to hardscrabble Pennsylvania coal miners, better call your product "root beer" instead of "root soda pop".
Harvey Mackay (on Charlie Hires)

A Virginia high school's course called "Home Economics for Boys" didn't generate much interest. Without changing the curriculum at all, the following year, it was listed as "Bachelor Living". It was packed.

If you do decide to make a 200-page business card as suggested above, make sure it has a spectacular name. A couple of psychologists, Golinkoff and Hirsh-Pasek, wrote a book on how children learn. I read a lot about kids when mine were younger. (Now, I just feed 'em once a week and hope for the best.) Their book, *Einstein Never Used Flashcards*, would have attracted my attention far more than a book called *How Children Learn*.

Can you imagine if Dr. John Gray's book had been called *Man/Woman Relationships in the 90s*, instead of *Men are From Mars, Women Are From Venus*?

There's a TV show in the New York City area that features a Priest (the Monsignor) and a Rabbi talking about stuff. There are plenty of marginal talk shows on TV with a religious theme, but I doubt many have 12 million viewers. Could it have something to do with the name of the show? It's called *The God Squad*. That's what I'm talking about. Brilliant!

Need some help coming up with a name? Check out Sam Horn's fabulous book *POP* for ideas.

Master of My Domain

A word about domain names. I have 503 at last count and only a handful of web sites. My friends are ready to send me to Domain Name Addicts Anonymous, but I stand my ground. They're not making any more lakefront and they're not making any more .coms. Unless you want to be stuck with .us or some such thing, grab the domain name for any projects you might want to launch in the next few years. They're like options on land. You can always let 'em go in a year if you don't need them. I've had inquiries to buy one of mine. It may be a stretch to call them an investment, but some domain names sell for tens of thousands of dollars or more. It's reported that *sex.com* sold for 12 million dollars U.S., making *business.com* seem like a deal at $7.5 million. Certainly, they can be priceless for your future business projects.

When you're naming your business, check first if the domain name is available. If it's taken, you may have a competitor out there you should check into.

Trademarks are also very valuable, but expensive and time consuming to obtain. Though they don't replace a trademark, for less than 10 bucks a pop, domain names are one of the best deals going to help reinforce the presence of your business.

So, you've cast yourself in the role you want, figured out what you're selling, developed and named your character. This show is really coming together. To protect what you've built, there's an important crew member I'd like you to meet.

CONTINUITY: GUARDIAN
OF THE BRAND

*O*n the set of any film or TV show, there's a person whose job is called simply "Continuity". It's her job to take Polaroids of all the actors and sets before every take and make sure that if the guy's shirt was tucked in on Take 2, it's still tucked in on Take 12. This allows the editors to piece the movie together later without worrying about the audience finding inconsistencies.

Businesses need a Continuity Department also. Even the most loyal audience won't hesitate to alert you to a continuity problem by not buying your product, as Coke found out at great expense!

You need continuity in how you look, in your printed materials, in your web site and in what you say in public (and sometimes, as presidents and TV personalities have found out the hard way, in what you say when you *think* you're in private). It's impossible to develop a public persona without some kind of continuity because you're not giving your audience enough clues to remember you.

Have you ever seen small news items on the Internet or in the paper, "50 Year Hollywood Veteran Dies"? You check out the article wondering who it is and when you see the name you don't recognize it, even after they give you a list of movies the guy played in. Queen Latifah, Billy Crystal, Hugh Grant, Robert DeNiro, each has carved out a persona so that we know what to expect. If you see the name Will Ferrell attached to a movie, you know it's going to be a stupid movie. If Ben Kingsley's in it, it'll be an epic. Even Madonna has carved out a persona as an iconoclastic vixen. What we expect from her is to be surprised; we expect the unexpected.

Playing Against Type

Your persona doesn't have to be one dimensional. Action heroes, Arnold Schwarzenegger, Vin Diesel and Sylvester Stallone, have all made big bucks on "Tough Guy Makes Nice" movies, where they break the "Never Follow Kids and Dogs" rule and show us their softer sides. These movies have a huge appeal for the same reason the "Behind the Scenes" shows and magazines like *People* are so popular. It's always fascinating to uncover an extra dimension to something you're already interested in.

You can't intrigue people by playing against type unless you've firmly established a type to play against.

But note that you can't intrigue people by playing against type unless you've firmly established a type to play against.

Before you commit to a persona for yourself or your company, make very sure it fits you. Then play it for all it's worth!

On Screen and Off
....

In Woody Allen's film, *The Purple Rose of Cairo*, Jeff Daniels plays a character who steps in and out of the movie screen. In real life, it's a lot harder to make this transition. The key to making a smooth transition is that your "on screen" persona has to be rooted in your real persona. It has to be authentic, only, "kicked up a notch" and accentuated, so people can see it.

In show business, an actor or singer's onstage persona is often vastly different than off stage. I once saw Tina Turner being interviewed on TV. The woman conducts herself like a well-dressed, well-bred conservative head of the local PTA. She could easily have tea and crumpets with Hillary Clinton or the Queen of England. On stage, she's a vamp.

This doesn't work well in business. You'll be considered a fake. Find a persona for yourself and your business that stems from something authentic in you and make that your on screen character. This'll make it easier for you to step into the spotlight. It won't feel like an unnatural step.

Ben and Jerry's did this beautifully. Two non-athletic types (they describe themselves as the "widest in their gym class") decide to go into the ice cream business (bagel machinery was too expensive) and change the face of capitalism. Their business became an arena for the implementation of their social values.

Do You Play What Your Audience Wants to Hear?
....

In the music industry, there are all sorts of books on how to write a hit song. Beyond verse, chorus, verse, chorus, bridge..., what do you have to do to get yourself a hit?

Musicians study these books in the hopes of writing the next smash hit song. Only the next hit usually comes from left field, from someone we've never heard of, someone who's doing his own thing. It's the same in the publishing industry and the movie industry.

Do you want to follow a formula and throw your hat in the ring with thousands of other formula followers, or do you want to take the risk of dancing to your own drum?

Not always an easy question to answer. On the one hand, you don't want to alienate your audience. I remember an episode of *The Apprentice* in which The Donald fired a project manager, partially because her team hired an inappropriate comedian for an event. On the other hand, it reminded me of events where I was the inappropriate comedienne.

> *That so few now dare to be eccentric, marks the chief danger of the time.*
>
> John Stuart Mill

We all have to decide. Do we want to be "appropriate for the event" or do we want to get known for what we do and let appropriate events find us? Would we still know Lenny Bruce's name if he were "appropriate for the event"?

Given the choice, and we all are, I'd choose to sing my song and let my audience find me.

> *Be yourself. Who else is better qualified?*
>
> Frank J. Giblin

When I started my coaching practice, I really didn't fit in at the business events I attended. But I resisted the pressure to conform and that's why my business succeeded. The crazy part is I now get testimonial letters from non-clients who say they've improved their performances just by observing me.

If you are different, *viva la difference*! If there are no real differences between you and your competition, create some.

Craft a unique character for you and your business, a persona based on who you really are and live it and breathe it consistently, so that you'll be seen and remembered. Give your audience something to hang on to.

Once you know you're being seen, you gotta make sure you're being heard.

CHAPTER 4

"Is This Thing On?"

ARE YOU BEING HEARD?

*W*alk into any comedy club in America on Open Mike Night and chances are you'll catch a struggling not-necessarily-young comedian dying on stage. As the guy stares out at the sea of blank faces, he taps on the microphone and utters the classic cliché, "Is this thing on?"

Walk into any Chamber of Commerce Networking Breakfast in America at 7:30 A.M. and you'll see the same ocean of blank faces as Johnny Entrepreneur introduces his business:

"Hi. I'm John Smyth of Borme Somemoreme and Snore. My company specializes in the facilitation of long-term pro-active soft skills solutions and strategies in the corporate environment. I'm the project manager... We're a one stop shop for small to medium-sized businesses... Our clients say that we provide excellent customer service. The services we provide are...excellent. Oh yeah, and we have 35 years experience doing that. We're located at the corner of..."

"BLAH, BLAH, BLAH..."

Hitting the Snooze Button

Remember the old Peanuts TV specials when the teacher speaks to Charlie Brown in class? All we hear is "blah, blah, blah, blah, blah".

It's unbelievable to me how many business people introduce themselves like that. The goal is to cut through the noise, not add to it!

I often open my speaking engagements with a spoof introduction like the one above. A few people get it, but you should see the pained expressions on the faces of the rest of 'em who think that they're going to have to listen to 45 minutes of that! Once I come clean, they breathe a sigh of relief and have a good laugh. But what many of them don't realize is that they sound just like that.

What to Say and How to Say It

In my house, we didn't miss an episode of *The Apprentice*. Whether you like him or not, The Trumpster knows how to play the star. Who else would have trumpets heralding his entrance to the boardroom and a throne on which to set his patootie?

In one of the episodes, The Donald fires this chick, Angie, because she messed up her presentation to a bunch of clothing executives, just because she "choked". No matter where you fall on the "Does he wear a toupee or doesn't he?" issue, you've got to admit — the guy's got a point.

It doesn't matter if you're the best darn accountant this side of the Tallahassee River. In business, if you don't know what to say and how to say it, forget about it. You're done. You might as well take your marbles and go home!

Presidencies have been won and lost on showmanship. An uncomfortable stiff candidate can kiss the White House goodbye. How's that for an inconvenient truth?

30 Seconds of Fame

And don't believe everything you hear. Business people love to tell you "It's all about long-term relationships. You can't get new clients in 30 seconds."

Well it ain't necessarily so. I attract more than half of my clients in just 30 seconds. And it's not just the *Vogue* supermodel looks, although there is that...

It's 'cause I knew from TV commercials that you could. It's like that four-minute mile thing.

For thousands of years, men knew that it was impossible, physically impossible, to run a four-minute mile. Only no one told Roger Bannister. So in 1954, he did it. Forty-six days later, another guy did it. A year later, 300 other people did it.

Let me be your Roger Bannister. You *can* get a client in 30 seconds. For me the "long-term relationship" starts *after* they become my client.

Romeo said "Let lips do what hands do". Shakespeare understood the power of words to seduce.

Turn on the Tube

Look how much TV commercials communicate in just 30 seconds. Our parents were always telling us to watch

Make your "infomercials" less "info" and more "mercial"!

less TV and do something useful with our time. But for entrepreneurs, watching TV commercials is great training.

How do we do better "infomercials" for our business? Make them less "info" and more "mercial"! It's a show. A mini show. All business is show business!

The 3 Ds of Opening Your Mouth in Public

In business, as in show business, there are 3 basic rules for attracting an audience.
1. Don't bore 'em
2. Don't bore 'em
And for G-d's sake:
3. Don't bore 'em!

Just because you're in business, doesn't mean you have to be boring!

You can't bore people into buying.
David Ogilvy

Don't Let Them Turn the Channel on You!
....

It's like your audience has a remote. So when the real estate agent tells you: "Now is a really great time to buy or sell a house, 'cause mortgage rates are low..."

Be honest. What do you do? You pull out your remote and either stick her on mute (while you think about what you're going to say) or you say "Next!" and turn the channel on her altogether.

Be a Tough Act to Follow!
....

In comedy duos, one guy is usually the straight man. His job is to set up the other guy for the punchline. Make sure *you're* not the straight man.

It's like that volleyball thing. The spike. You throw it up in the air and the other guy slams it over the net. What you're really doing is setting up a great opportunity for anyone smart enough to grab it. The more boring *you* are, the more interesting someone else seems. You set it up; he scores. Great for team sports and comedy duos, but in business you don't want to be someone else's foil.

When I'm in an "around the room introduction" situation, I'm not satisfied till I get my usual "Well, that's a tough act to follow" comment from the next guy.

How do you get that? You gotta get your act together.

There are two basic elements for a spectacular show. No, I'm not talking popcorn and milk duds, although that never hurts. You need to have a great script and a great performance.

THE SCRIPT

Yackety Yak
. . . .

*Y*ou're at a networking event.

Up stands Yackety Yackerson, followed by Blahy Blaherson and Yada Yada Yanderson. Then, it's time for the keynote speaker, Bormy Some Morrison.

How do you make sure you're not one of them?

Well, remember, ALL business is show business. Don't step onto the stage with a lousy script!

Be Careful What Words You Use

●●

*D*on't be using words like:
- technology
- effective
- solutions
- value propositions
- deliverables
- advanced
- best customer service
- module
- HR
- IT
- communications
- integrated
- corporate
- systems
- soft skills
- core competencies
- we service small to medium sized businesses
- for all your blah blah blah needs

What do these words have in common?
- They're colorless.
- There's no flavor.
- They're meaningless filler.
- We don't know what you mean.
- We don't believe you anyway.
- But most importantly, we can't see them!

Why do the telephone companies use cute little monkeys and frogs and geckos in their ads? Why? Because you can't see phone service.

We need to create a visual for our audience. We have to add color every time we open our mouths in public so people can *see* what we're saying. We have to create pictures with our words.

Lose the "Professionalitis"

Speak to the audience with the same kind of language and tone you'd use talking with your best friend (minus any @#&*#@!). Forget the corporate gobbledygook. And don't worry about sounding "professional".

By the way, when in doubt, ask a kid. Kids usually have a natural born immunity to corporate-speak till they reach their early 20s and land their first "real" job.

Don't Overeducate

In an infomercial situation, you only have about 30 seconds. Don't spend more than 5 seconds on information. Use the rest to convey a feeling.

After about eight months on the business networking circuit, I kept hearing about "critical illness insurance", mainly from this one insurance agent who spent most of her time promoting it. Finally, I realized that it was a great product and I bought it.

But not from her. I bought it from another insurance agent, just 'cause I liked him. So what good did it do her spending all her time hucking critical illness insurance? She should have been selling herself too.

You have other things to communicate in addition to the benefits of your product, things like warmth, trust, credibility, likeability...

Let's Slip into Something More Comfortable

I read a television production book that discussed planning camera shots. It told the story of a full-production TV show that decided to scale back to a one-man, one-camera show. The result? Both viewership and sponsorship increased.

In a world of "razzle dazzle 'em", this is surprising. The producer's take on it was that the change made the programme warmer and more intimate. The format forced the performer to project more intimately because he couldn't rely on the production to help him connect.

No amount of technology, no amount of slick, no amount of glitz, no amount of professionalism can hold a candle to the power of creating a real connection.

The "So What?" Factor

When we speak, our audience is scanning our speeches, much like the metal detectors you see scanning the beach on a summer evening. The beach people are looking for gold rings that may have been lost and buried in the sand. Your audience is looking for golden nuggets of wisdom, for relevance to their lives or their businesses. If they don't immediately detect the relevance, they say, or more often only think, "so what?" If you don't spontaneously answer that question for your audience, i.e., answer it before they ask it, you've given them a perfect reason to turn the channel on you.

Remote Control

There's a reason they call it a remote control. Who ever has the remote, has the control.

So give them the answer, but be careful how you do. Don't bang 'em over the head with it.

> There's a reason they call it a remote control. Who ever has the remote, has the control.

Shopping for Benefits

Contrary to what they teach in Marketing 101, don't be giving us a shopping list of your benefits. What kind of a lousy script is that? Me, I'd rather spend two hours in the dentist chair listening to Barry Manilow than trapped in a room full of people spouting out their benefits all over the place!

These are often the same people who'll force feed you a brochure or two or ten, just in case you want to rush home and read more about their business and maybe take a few pamphlets around to your neighbors after dinner.

Don't feel stupid if you've done it. We've all done it. I've done it. But it doesn't make sense! It's *not* what attracts people to you or your business.

It's not what makes you a star! We need to learn to entice, not chase, new clients.

Don't Say You're the Best. Why?

'Cause

1. Everyone says it.
2. It's probably not true.
3. We don't believe you anyway.
   But don't worry about it. Why? Because
4. We don't necessarily hire the best.

We're Not Always Looking for the Best

A few years ago, I was looking for a photographer to do my actor's headshots and also some shots for my CD promotion. A bunch of photographers sent me samples of their work. The one I ended up choosing was not, in my opinion, the best. So why did I choose her?

'Cause I liked her on the phone. She was excited about my project and sounded not only enthusiastic but very flexible and ready to run around with me to beaches and even scout out locations. That's what *she* was selling. Enthusiasm. Flexibility. I got a great shot which I made into a postcard and I ended up referring my clients to her.

Maybe we want the nicest, the most easy going, the warmest, most colorful, most flexible, most unique...

We're Not Attracted to Perfection!

Look at singers. Often the most famous, the most loved are not the best. Rod Stewart. What's that all about? The guy's like 92 and still churning out hit albums!

Who's sexier, a male department store suit model or Johnny Depp? I rest my case.

In Chapter 3, we talked about what you're really selling and I did this fancy shmancy *shpiel* about Coke and

Harley. But let me tell you, what you're really selling is you. One hundred percent you.

Joe Girard, who can legitimately call himself the Greatest Salesman in the World since the Guinness World Book of Records gave him that title 12 years in a row, agrees. Girard says he owes his success to that simple philosophy.

You're selling you. Especially when you're an entrepreneur. (By the way, it's easier to be a star if you think of yourself as an entrepreneur — even if your employer is your only client.) You're on the front lines. What you see is what you get. Let's hope they like what they're seeing.

You're not going to get 'em to like you by professing your sincerity.

> *Everyone says he's sincere, but everyone isn't sincere. If everyone was sincere who says he's sincere there wouldn't be half so many insincere ones in the world and there would be lots, lots, lots more really sincere ones!*
> Tennessee Williams

You have to show them. Obviously, you don't want to have to wait till they're customers to show 'em because that'd put you in the classic Catch 22 situation. But you do have to demonstrate it with your words.

Don't State the Obvious
••••••••••••••••••••••••••••••

By the way, saying: "You'll know how to use your computer better after taking our computer training" is like saying "You'll have more groceries after shopping at our grocery store" or "Your hair will be shorter after you've come to our salon for a haircut".

As my kids would say, "Duh!"

You're wasting the few seconds of attention you have before they turn the channel.

SCENE 2

What Is The Business Script Missing?

What Is Show Business?

I've said that all business is show business. But what is show business? What's a song, a movie, a play, an opera, even a ballet?

It's a story. That's what the business script is missing. The Story.

The Story

How do you add stories to your business? Add them to your speeches, your infomercials, how you dress, your business name, your brochure.

Why add them? Because stories create intimacy. They're captivating. And they create a connection between you and your audience. But most importantly, they keep people interested. On your channel. Ever see a movie without a plot? Bet you didn't stick around for the credits.

> What Is Show Business? It's a story. That's what the business script is missing. The Story.

103

Where Do You Find These Stories?

You have to go digging for them.

You dig for color and flavor and before you know it, you will have unearthed a story. Sometimes literally...

Color Me Red

One of my clients had to give a fairly dry "how to" speech to a group of professional speakers and she wasn't a professional speaker herself. She was nervous because the last few times she spoke in public, she felt she had bombed. So we went digging for color.

And we found it. On a tomato farm. Interviewing her, I found out she grew up on a tomato farm and had been picking tomatoes since she was eight years old, sorting them and helping her dad bring them to market.

Tomatoes are colorful! And it occurred to me that her job now was to pick speakers and bring them to market. So, we told her story of growing up on the farm and used a tomato analogy to make her point about speakers, how some are still too green, some are ripe and juicy and ready for market and some are just plain rotten!

But what if you don't have any color? You do! You just have to dig for it.

She said there was a line up of people waiting to speak to her afterwards. She was a hit! She didn't realize it, but the color had been there all along.

You need to use color every time you open your mouth. But what if you don't have any color?

You do! Everyone has it. You just have to dig for it. And everyone's got a story.

I just got off the phone with one of my editors, Karen. All our dealings so far have been on the phone, but I must admit when we first spoke, I was a little concerned that she might be a bit conservative to connect with my voice. After all, she grew up in Britain and was a member of the Potter's Guild. I misplaced her phone number, so I "googled" her and found a fascinating article she'd written about her year long stint moaning for money as a phone sex operator to repay her student loans.

Everybody's got a story. Find yours and have the courage to tell it.

The difference between stars and bit players often comes down to finding the courage to tell your story, having the confidence that your audience will find it interesting or entertaining.

Where does that confidence come from?

There's an old saying that "appetite comes with eating". Well I say, "Confidence comes with the telling." You may be taking a risk at first, but when you start to see your audience warm up to you, you'll know it was a risk worth taking. The spotlight is not going to shine on you unless you attract it.

What Kind of Storyteller Do You Want to Be?

*Y*ou've found your story. Soon, you're gonna learn how to tell it. But first, you have some decisions to make. You have to decide what kind of storyteller you want to be.

My kids told me a story recently. When my youngest daughter was five years old, her older sisters offered her a cranberry muffin. She tasted it, spit it out and said "Ew. Don't like cranberry!" So they offered her a strawberry muffin which she gobbled down with delight.

My kids are amazing marketers. All the muffins in that package were cranberry!

That's what I call the "Tell 'Em What They Wanna Hear" marketing approach. Very popular. And it works.

Here's Looking at You Kid!
••••••••••••••••••••••••••••••••••••••

Seth Godin writes about a manufacturer of expensive wine glasses who claims that wine tastes better in his uniquely shaped wine glasses than in $1 wine glasses. This manufacturer has the wine aficionados and even the wine magazines verifying his claim, despite scientific evidence that it makes absolutely no difference.

But in fact, wine *does* taste better in these wine glasses. Why? Because we think it does. The story becomes true because we believe it's true or in Godin's words, the manufacturer "makes your wine taste better by telling you a story."

Me, I prefer another type of marketing, kinda revolutionary and definitely not as popular. "The Truth".

Now I know we've all been taught to "Sell the sizzle, not the steak", and I must admit, you're not going to sell much if you call it "a slice of dead cow on a plate"! But the truth has its own seductive charm.

Don't be telling me that your cough syrup has a "great cherry flavor". When was the last time anyone tasted a great tasting cough syrup? Buckley's Mixture has a brilliant script. "It tastes awful. And it works!"

Credibility through the roof. They already admitted to us that it tastes awful. Why would they start lying to us now?

When in Doubt, Tell it Like it Is

A mortgage broker came to me to help her get noticed in networking situations. What struck me about her immediately was a weariness, a frustration that she wasn't connecting with the people she met at these meetings. And she wasn't placing enough mortgages.

> You're not going to sell much if you call it "a slice of dead cow on a plate"! But the truth has its own seductive charm.

107

The reason was obvious. She wasn't "feeling the love". Upon further prodding, she admitted that being a mortgage broker was something she just fell into. My first reaction was that she should find a profession that really turns her on. But she insisted that she had to make this work.

The next morning, I woke up at 6:10 A.M. and it hit me like a ton of bricks. "When in doubt, tell the truth". So I wrote her the following infomercial:

> *"I didn't become a mortgage broker because I love mortgages. Who loves mortgages? What I love is people. And shopping! I'm Josephine Blow. I became a mortgage broker because I love shopping and getting the best deal. I just bought a gorgeous Anne Klein suit and I didn't pay retail. I got it for 30% off. Wanna see what kind of deal I can get you? Josephine Blow. Mortgage Shopper. Why pay retail?"*

It's not Shakespeare, but it's going to be very comfortable for her to deliver because every word is true. Down to the brown pinstriped Anne Klein suit (which I suggested she return because it made her look like a boring mortgage broker).

Once again, business can learn from show business. After years of pablum, in the 70s, TV started to get real. Norman Lear's *All in the Family* became such a big hit because, for the first time in prime time, we saw our own dysfunctional family on the screen. We saw that we weren't alone, that someone else's father called his wife a "dingbat", his son-in-law a "meathead" and didn't let anyone sit in his chair, and was a bigot to boot.

Henry Beckwith, in his wonderful book, *Selling the Invisible*, demonstrates why we should "Show [Our] Warts". He tells of a study at a state university in which researchers made up two fictitious job candidates with identical resumes. The letters of reference which went to personnel directors were almost identical as well, except that one contained the additional phrase "Sometimes John can be difficult to get along with".

Most people would be surprised to hear that the candidate the directors most wanted to interview was, in Beckwith's words, "Sometimes-Difficult-To-Get-Along-With-John." I'm not surprised. John's letter was perceived as more credible than an all-glowing reference.

I get my testimonial letters from clients by having clients repeat their spontaneous compliments ("You're brilliant!", "You're awesome!") into a tape recorder. Once the tape is rolling, they sometimes joke and add that I'm "bossy" or "annoying". I love having the word "bossy" in there along with all the compliments. The prospects will know that my client is giving them the straight goods.

Years after *All in the Family*, showbiz once again broke new ground with "reality TV" shows, although how "real" they really are is up for debate. The point is that we're hungry for something more than what the old "breach of contract" legal cases used to call "puffery", a bunch of hot air about how great your product is. The truth. What a concept!

You have other decisions to make.

Would You Rather Be Loved or Feared?

In *A Bronx Tale*, Chazz Palmintieri's character is asked "Is it better to be loved or feared?" His persona as a local Mafia chief calls for him to be feared rather than loved.

If Chazz were playing Grandpa Walton or Smokey the Bear, the answer might have been different.

Ask yourself, what role do you want to play in the marketplace? And how do you want your audience to regard you? What do you want your audience to think and feel about you? What do you want your brand to be?

Al Pacino isn't looking for his audience to pal up to him the way Richard Simmons is. I wouldn't shake my bootie "Dancing to the Oldies" with Al any more than I would shake in my boots watching Richard in *Scarface*.

Different personas. Different markets.

When I give seminars on "Your 30 Seconds of Fame", how to do a sparkling 30 second infomercial, I get the participants to stand up and do their regular intro. I assign each of them a number and after we've been around the room, I call people up by number and I ask the rest of the people in the room what they remember about this person. Do they know the person's name? Do they remember his business? What else do they remember? It's surprising how little they remember and what's even more interesting is that what they do remember is how they felt about the person. They may not remember much, but they do remember whether they liked him or trusted him.

Shy participants are sometimes shocked to hear that the audience felt intimidated by them. Remarkably, shy people often register with others as being intimidating. (More on the shy thing below.) It's a very revealing exercise.

It's important to determine what traits would attract your audience to consider buying from you. As a lawyer, it didn't hurt if potential clients knew that I made the Dean's List and graduated 4th in my class at law school. Now as a coach, I'm more interested in showcasing my creativity and stage presence, the fact that I "get" what attracts people, the fact that I dish out the straight goods, more Simon than Paula.

What do you want people to know, think and feel about you? Do you want to emphasize your warmth, integrity, approachability, intelligence, expertise, wit, trustworthiness, humor or originality? Or maybe just that you're young and fearless?

"You Like Me, You Really Like Me"

Almost 25 years later, people still remember Sally Field's Oscar acceptance speech. Silly, maybe, but her vulnerability struck a chord. Because that's what we're all going for; we all want to be liked. And we like to do business with people we like. The most important skill an entrepreneur can learn is the business of being liked.

Speak in Your Own Voice

OK, so maybe I said it before, but I'm saying it again. Be yourself.

The Spotlight Finds Originals

Like a fly finds honey, like a cop finds donuts, like Dr. Phil finds book projects for his family, the spotlight finds originals. Don't copy anyone. Don't try to be anyone else. Speak in your own voice.

> *Like a cop finds donuts, the spotlight finds originals. Speak in your own voice.*

This isn't always easy, because for many of us, our own voice has been deeply buried, under layers and layers of how we think we're supposed to sound. But we gotta find it, if we ever hope to be heard, if we ever hope to stand out. Writers and musicians are told this all the time, but it applies to everyone, especially entrepreneurs.

Be true to your own voice. I had a client who spoke like she'd swallowed a dictionary — I'm talkin' a 16-volume, first edition, Oxford English Dictionary. She didn't know how to speak any other way. Instead of trying to make her sound "normal", or the way people speak nowadays, which probably wouldn't have worked anyway, I suggested that we make her manner of speech part of her "shtick". The only embellishment was that she would occasionally shock her audience with a very current reference, so that she'd get a laugh and they'd know that it was *her* show.

What's Your Schtick?

Those who dismiss Dolly Parton as just mammaries and a blonde wig, just don't get it. I admit I was once one of them, till a friend dragged me to a packed stadium, many years ago, to see her in action. Much like "I fell off the turnip truck" *American Idol* contestant Kelly Pickler, Dolly knows what she's doing. The woman embraces her authentic "Aw shucks, smokey mountain, coat of many colors" roots, kicks it up a notch so everyone can see it and sings all the way to the bank. More power to her.

Finding your own voice is key for success.

SCENE 4

How Do You Write a Blockbuster Script?

*O*K. Welcome to Scriptwriting 101. This ain't what they taught you at Salesman School.

The Written Word Is Different from the Spoken Word
....

Before you even start to write, you gotta get into the right frame of mind. Otherwise, whatever you prepare on paper won't work in front of an audience.

We speak differently than we write. Less formally. People don't speak with proper sentence structure. At least, not when they're comfortable. I coach my clients to speak to audiences like they're speaking to their best friend on the phone, with their feet up. It creates intimacy and makes it more likely the audience will seek you out afterwards.

Speaking in public is like playing the violin. You have to vary the volume, the tone, the pitch, the rhythm and the tempo. It also doesn't hurt to whisper once in a while. Any change in how you address your audience will grab attention.

Spy on people speaking to each other when they don't know you're watching. You'll find people do these things naturally, till they notice they have an audience.

Write Your Own Screenplay

Movies are often based on novels or even short stories. But they don't make a movie directly from a novel. They hire someone to write a screenplay. Unlike novels, and most speeches, the words in a screenplay or a play are written in the script the way they're meant to be spoken, along with stage directions in brackets.

When I write a speech for myself, I write "You gotta" instead of "You have to" or "You must", because that's the way I'm going to ("gonna") say it. I've even written most of this book that way, with just enough inconsistency to make sure I don't violate my "we're not looking for perfection" rule. This book is full of sentence fragments. Why? 'Cause I want you to hear the way I speak when you're reading it.

One of the most common mistakes business people make, when asked to speak, is writing the speech the way they would write a report or an article. Spoken language is very different than written language.

Here's one of my favorite tricks. I say what I'm writing out loud to myself as I'm writing it. Then I adjust anything that doesn't feel comfortable coming out of my mouth.

Use Words as Props

Certain words or phrases will always get an audience's attention. Especially out of context. "Broccoli" is one of them.

I rarely make a speech without referring to broccoli and I usually even bring some. (Makes a good healthy door prize.) It doesn't matter that it has nothing to do with anything. I always find a way to make it fit and always get a laugh. I even wrote a song about my mother that has broccoli in the title ("Broccoli's on Sale at Dominion"). It's one of my most requested radio songs, especially on Mother's Day.

"Hillbilly Flamenco"

Speaking of music, I was at an international music conference and I caught a few minutes of a session with the head of CD Baby, Derek Sivers. He told a great story about a band whose music had once been described by an audience member as "Hillbilly Flamenco". Adding that eclectic description to the band's promo materials was enough to send CD sales through the roof. I'm guessing most of the people who bought the CD were not huge fans of either musical genre but the unique combination of words was enough to make people curious. Curiosity attracts.

Curiosity itself is not enough to sustain success. Once the public's curiosity is satisfied, they'll move on to the next novelty. Still, the odd label serves two functions. It gets the audience there in the first place and if people do like the music, it gives them something unique to say as they pass the name

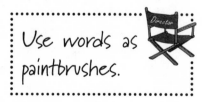

Use words as paintbrushes.

on. The coolness of it is contagious. It makes the news spreader feel and sound "in the know". If you're lucky, these things sprout up spontaneously and spread by themselves. More often, you'll need to help spread them. More about that in Chapter 5.

Create Characters

One way to make your script memorable is to create characters for your stories and name them. Instead of saying "I met a guy", tell us that his name is "Joe". Instead of telling us about your teacher in grade two, give her a name, Sister Mary Catharine. By the way, you can't go wrong with nuns in your stories. Even Elvis made a movie with nuns. I don't make up the rules!

When in doubt, throw in some nuns!

Give your characters a profession. Tell us what they look like. Make 'em real, so we can see them.

Set the Scene

Paint a picture. Use words as paintbrushes. Make the scene colorful!

Let's face it. Legal judgments aren't very sexy. Right up there with financial statements and income tax regulations. *"The party of the first part engaged the party of the second part…"* And yet a British Judge, Lord Denning, made his judgments come alive by peppering them with stories and colorful language. It's been a few years, so I'm totally making this up, but they went something like this…

> *It was a lovely spring day in Canterbury. The birds were singing and little Jimmy Reilly was out playing cricket in his backyard when all of a sudden a croquet ball from the neighboring club flew over the fence and hit Jimmy on the head knocking the poor lad unconscious.*

Then, Lord Denning went on to decide the case, but he captured his audience's interest in a way that few judges have before or since.

Best Place to Start a Story?

Next time you watch a great movie, pay attention to how it starts. You're usually thrown right into the middle of something and then you try to fit the pieces together.

Do like the movies do. Grab 'em! Start right in the middle.

"So I'm sitting in the back of the taxi cab...Sister Mary Catharine's banging on the window..." (Make your characters recurring characters for extra laughs.)

You gotta know what's going to happen next!

Tell the Story in the Present Tense

> Grab 'em! Start right in the middle.

If you watch comedians, you'll note that they tell their stories in the present tense. "So I'm standing there..." It creates more immediacy. Your audience is right there with you, almost like it's happening to them.

Create Suspense!

You know when you're flipping through the channels to see what's on and you get caught on those *ET* Birthdays? *Entertainment Tonight* shows you three guys in silhouette, gives you a clue and challenges you to figure out which of the three "I-haven't-had-a-hit-in-years" guys is having a birthday. Then, they go to commercial.

It's not like you care whether it's Keanu Reeves or the *Miami Vice* guy, but they've made you curious! So you stay on their channel two minutes longer and wait through the endless commercials, because if you turn the channel, you'll miss it. You're caught in their wicked web. The mind hates an incomplete puzzle.

You're caught in their wicked web. The mind hates an incomplete puzzle.

Look what Cadbury did. "How do you get the caramel in a Caramilk Bar?" I used to wonder about that for days as a kid. Had to experiment with a lot of chocolate bars to try to figure it out! How 'bout the secret Coca-Cola formula or KFC's 11 secret herbs and spices? The late Colonel's recipe is locked in a safe in Louisville, Kentucky. Suspense attracts the spotlight.

Take 'Em "Behind the Scenes"

Entertainment Tonight spawned a whole industry of "behind the scenes" journalism. We love finding out what stars do in their spare time, how on-screen lovers actually hated each other and how Harrison Ford used to be a carpenter.

Take your prospects behind the scenes in your business. Tell 'em why you're doing what you're doing and how you came to be doing it. Clients love my "litigation lawyer leaves law for limelight" story just as I love reading how Ray Kroc, of McDonald's fame, was a milkshake machine salesman when he came upon the McDonald brothers, how Colonel Sanders was about to retire on a small government social security check when he started Kentucky Fried Chicken and how the richest man in the world, Bill Gates, was a college dropout. And people spread these stories and they start to have a life of their own.

You Confuse, You Lose

If you give a reference or tell a joke that the audience doesn't understand, you make 'em feel dumb, inadequate. The result? They won't like you because they associate you with that feeling of inadequacy.

The opposite is also true. Often I "forget" a word and have the audience help me out, so they feel involved. OK, so it's a trick used with toddlers, but before you dismiss it as condescending and manipulative, try it. It works.

The Power of Personality

I once helped an accountant with her networking introduction. Her manner, in public, was cold, unapproachable and intimidating, very staccato and to the point, and chock full of info. I wrote her an infomercial playing on how she sounded like an automaton, allowing her to gently tease herself and show some personality in the process. A month or so later, she told me this story.

She was at a chamber of commerce networking meeting where another accountant stood up and gave information including the fact that he consulted on Quick Books. She just focused on showing her personality. After the meeting, a woman came up to her and asked if she did Quick Books. She did and so she got the job. Why her? The other guy said he did it. Why? Because she attracted.

What's the moral of the story? The moral is — if an accountant can do it, anyone can!

(I sometimes worry when I'm speaking to a group of business people that I'm going to get mugged in the alley afterwards by a gang of irate accountants. But that's the very good thing about accountants. You don't have to cross the street late at night to avoid them. Have you ever heard about a mugging by some guy named Sheldon or Leslie? What's he gonna do? Get you with his pocket protector? I said something similar recently during a keynote speech and an accountant yelled out, "Nah, You won't get mugged; you'll get audited!")

Business is a seduction!

We need to entice not chase. Business is a seduction!

One way to seduce 'em is with humor.

Humor Is Not a Four Letter Word

I get a lot of mileage out of my humor, but many of my clients, even those who were originally attracted to me because of it, get queasy when I suggest the "H" word for them.

My Business is Serious

"But, Tsufit, my business is serious!" Clients tell me this all the time, like I spent 10 years with the Barnum and Bailey Circus instead of practicing law in a downtown office tower. I've coached directors of child abuse agencies, funeral directors, bereavement counselors... Humor works with all of them.

Make 'Em Laugh

Humor loosens people up and gets you past their defense system, the guard dog, the gatekeeper that says "I ain't buying nothin' from her!"

Humor is disarming. It helps you penetrate and make your point to an unreceptive audience. It's always been that way. In *Ask For The Moon and Get It!*, Percy Ross tells the story of George Washington opposing a resolution to restrict the U.S. standing army to 5000 troops. Washington told his opponents that he had no problem with the 5000 soldier limit if they "would also limit the size of any invading army to 3000 men". Humor helped him make his point.

One recent participant in my infomercials seminar got up to do her 30 second intro for my critique. She spoke about the dangers of electromagnetic emissions from cell phones, a problem, for which she claimed to have a solution. I asked the audience, afterwards, how they felt about this woman. Most people admitted that they felt intimidated and put off by her preaching. I suggested to her that humor could be used to make the same point. She was a great student and showed up the next day, in front of a different group, and got applause for her performance.

Humor is the perfect tool when communicating about a serious subject. I heard a joke which apparently originated in the former Soviet Union. A guy orders an automobile and is told that he can come to pick up his car in exactly 10 years. The customer asks, "In the morning or afternoon?" The salesclerk asks, "In 10 years, what's the difference?" "Well", the guy says, "The plumber is coming in the morning". How better to communicate frustration about long wait times?

Humor also allows you to say things you might not otherwise dare say. It takes the edge off. There's an urban legend about a hairdresser that was actually re-enacted by an entrepreneur I know, Diane. Now the head of a networking organization, Diane tells the story of when she owned a hair salon in a small town. Diane made a habit of welcoming new entrepreneurs to town, so when a competitor opened across the street, she invited him out to lunch. They had a great chat and Diane made only one small request: "Do anything you want, but please don't undercut me on price." The next day, her new competitor stuck a sign in his window that said "We give $6.95 haircuts." Without missing a beat, Diane, put up a cheerful sign in her window that said "We fix $6.95 haircuts!"

What If I'm Not Funny?

"But, Tsufit, what if I'm not funny?" I get this question a lot.

Humor is more than just jokes. In *Punchline*, an 80s movie set in a comedy club, Sally Field plays a New Jersey housewife who steals her family's cookie jar money, 500 big ones, to buy 25 jokes to use at the club. The dough would have been better used for cookies. Her gags get her nothing more than the occasional chuckle till she gets taken under the wing of the Tom Hanks character who tells her to lose the jokes and just talk to the audience. About herself. Her life. He teaches her that "Everybody's funny". Lo and behold, she finds her voice, the audience laughs and everyone lives happily ever after.

A joke is to humor what pornography is to erotic language.

James Humes

Humor is a way of being, an honesty in the way you speak and observe. Remember "Broccoli's on Sale at Dominion", my song about my mother's long distance telephone advice:

Don't drink Coca-Cola. Caffeine makes you nervous.
You know I don't give advice. But don't buy dishes.
I've got lots. I'll bring you. I got them all half price.

123

I've had Filipinos, Hungarians, Koreans come up to me after I sing it. "That's *my* mom." Actually, Italians make some of the best Jewish mothers. "Hey Rico, why you no finish your spaghetti?"

What's funny about it is how universally true it is. (OK, so maybe this is my second mention of the Broccoli song. Since when is it a crime to move a bit of product? Four kids, braces, college...)

Humor is observation about life's truths. Humor is also an openness. Humor is color. If you can throw in a bit of wit, so much the better. Most people are funny sometimes. They're just afraid to do it in public.

I have a client who's a funeral director. She says, "I'm funny on weekends!" What a waste! Another one of my funeral director clients (I have almost enough funeral directors to order matching T-shirts), she's a hoot-and-a-half while still communicating her compassion and sincerity.

Don't Send in the Clowns

If you go to business networking functions (which you should), you may be encouraged to use corny taglines (which you shouldn't). "Memory Hooks", as top networking organization BNI calls them, are a great idea but proceed with caution. A lot of them get pretty cheesy. I won't list any examples here, because I don't want to offend the people using them, but you've heard them too. Just remember: "Funny, good. Goofy, bad." If it has nothing to do with what you do, don't say it just to make a bad pun. I'll give you a list of great lines later in this chapter.

> *Just remember:*
> *"Funny, good.*
> *Goofy, bad."*

A Comic Says Funny Things and a Comedian Says Things Funny

There's more than one way to get a laugh.

My kids used to watch the TV show *Everyone Loves Raymond*, starring comedian Ray Romano. I noticed that Ray doesn't really say anything funny. It's just that everything he says and does, down to even his facial expressions, elicits a laugh. He reminds me of Jackie Gleason in the vintage *The Honeymooners* shows. One glance and his audience was rolling in the aisles. Some comedians, like Steven Wright, get laughs by saying everything in a deadpan monotone voice. Exaggerating traits you already have is enough to get you a laugh.

I once got "one upped" by an accountant (damn those accountants!!) who did just that. We were at a networking meeting. I had just mesmerized them with my sparkling 30 seconds. On previous occasions, this accountant had been deadly boring. But this time, she was brilliant. She exaggerated how boring she was to the extent that it became very funny. Her deadpan delivery got a bigger laugh than I did.

Use Detail

I read somewhere that a comedian was complaining to a fellow comedian that his joke, about a dog falling from a building, wasn't working. He wasn't getting any laughs.

So, the more experienced comedian tells him, "Make the dog a German Shepherd." And whatdya know? The joke worked. The guy got his laugh. Detail helps. We've got to be able to *see* what you're saying!

The Squash Book only sold 1500 copies, but *The Zucchini Cookbook* (same book, different name and cover) sold

125

300,000 copies. Details add color. Details also add credibility. Procter & Gamble must have realized that "99 and 44/100% Pure" is a much better slogan than "100% Pure" for Ivory Soap.

And They'll Tell Two Friends and So On...

I'm not saying it's easy. Any comedian will tell you comedy is hard work. Check out Jerry Seinfeld's 2002 documentary *Comedian* to see just how hard. But like most things worth having, it's worth the effort. Using humor in your presentations makes it more likely that what you say will be repeated by your audience to others, increasing your exposure.

Most people appreciate this color, flavor and humor in others, yet they recoil from adding it to their own presentations. Why? I don't think it's the work people are afraid of. My theory is that even though most people secretly long to get noticed, they're actually embarrassed to stand out. It's up to you.

You don't have to incorporate humor into your presentations (or your marketing) any more than you have to incorporate broccoli into your diet. But, as my mom says, it's good for you.

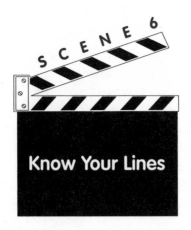

SCENE 6

Know Your Lines

Have Your Own Lines

tars have their own language, their own way of speaking and their own lines. Have your own sayings. Nothing catches on like a good, often repeated line. Remember the Wendy's commercial, "Where's the beef?" Voting someone "Off the island" from *Survivor*?

I have my own "Tsufitisms", like "Approach the Bench" whenever I beckon someone to come speak intimately with me. People always laugh because they know I was a lawyer and they've watched enough courtroom dramas on TV to know that it means the judge is going to have a personal "off the record" word with counsel.

Another one of my favorites: "Thanks for sharing", borrowed from the Twelve-Step programmes and used whenever anyone says anything gruesome, inappropriate or graphic. Never fails to get a laugh. If I feel I've been monopolizing the conversation (who me?), I usually interrupt myself and say "But enough about you!" It's not planned or deliberate, but these lines are always in my pocket, ready to break the ice and they add color to my persona.

Dr. Phil has "How's that working out for you?" and "Love Smart" which not so coincidentally is the name of a book that sells more copies every time one of his guests uses the term "loving smart" or "loving dumb". Nothing dumb about that.

Joan Rivers' trademark line "Can We Talk?" is actually that, a federally registered trademark!

What are your lines? You probably have a few. Better if they're yours. Teenagers usually say whatever's popular on TV, movies or commercials (remember "Show me the money" or "My bad"?), but it's nice if you can develop your own. Here are a few classic lines to get you started. See if you can guess which lines sell what.

What's My Line?

"We try harder."
"Think small."
"The ultimate driving machine."
"The antidote for civilization."
"When it absolutely, positively has to be there overnight."
"Finger lickin' good."
"Because I'm worth it."
"You'll wonder where the yellow went."
"All the news that's fit to print."
"Let your fingers do the walking."
"Reach out and touch someone."
"The quicker picker-upper."
"A little dab'll do ya."
"Have it your way."
"It's everywhere you want to be."
"Drivers wanted."
"A diamond is forever."
"When you care enough to send the very best."

"Snap! Crackle! Pop!"

"I love New York."

"Virginia is for lovers."

"Good to the last drop."

"Please don't squeeze the _____."

"Breakfast of Champions."

"Ring around the collar."

"Mmm, mm good."

"This Bud's for you."

"Look, Ma! No cavities."

"Takes a licking and keeps on ticking."

"_____ tastes good, like a cigarette should."

"Strong enough for a man, but made for a woman."

"You can take _____ out of the country, but you can't
   take the country out of _____."

"You deserve a break today."

"Let's ask Mikey."

"Built for drivers."

"Fly the friendly skies."

• • •

Answers
············

Avis, Volkswagen, BMW, Club Med, Federal Express,
KFC, L'Oréal, Pepsodent, The New York Times, Yellow
Pages, AT&T, Bounty, Brylcreem, Burger King, Visa,
Volkswagen, De Beers Consolidated, Hallmark, Kellogg's
Rice Krispies, New York, Virginia, Maxwell House coffee,
Charmin toilet tissue, Wheaties cereal, Wisk detergent,
Campbell's soup, Budweiser beer, Crest toothpaste, Timex
watch, Winston cigarettes, Secret antiperspirant, Salem
cigarettes, McDonalds, Life cereal, Pontiac Sunfire,
United Airlines

Interrupt!!!!

f you were brought up in a "seen but not heard" household, this may seem jarring for you, but that's what marketing is. An interruption. Find a way to incorporate interruption into your scripts.

I come from a long line of interrupters. Some find it irritating, but it does get attention. If you don't interrupt, you don't get your turn. The trick is to make the interruption welcome, to make it a "surprise" rather than an interruption.

The noisier it gets, the more ingenious you have to be about how to interrupt. It doesn't have to be noisy. In fact, noise is the first thing that gets filtered out. It just has to break through, interrupt a pattern.

Kindergarten teachers turn off the lights to interrupt a room full of noisy five year olds. A person walking into

> *The trick is to make the interruption welcome, to make it a "surprise" rather than an interruption.*

a boardroom meeting in a bikini interrupts. I was once hiking in the Ein Gedi Nature Reserve, near the Dead Sea and the Judean Desert. (Yeah, hiker girl, that's me.) At its lowest point, 400 feet below sea level, it's the lowest point in the world. After trekking deeper and deeper into the reserve for two hours and bathing in waterfalls, the landscape was interrupted by the unlikely sight of a full symphony orchestra, I'm talkin' tuxedos, cellos, oboes, the whole bit. We later found out they had made the impossible descent, one at a time, by helicopter. Now that's an interruption!

There's a movement towards opt-in or "permission marketing". It's a great idea, but you still gotta interrupt to get their permission to interrupt.

Commercials are an interruption. Or at least they used to be.

"And Now, a Message from Our Sponsor"

Used to be that there was a line between the TV show and the commercial. During the show, you sat on the couch with a bag of chips. During the commercials, you ran to beat the rest of the family to the washroom and grab some more chips. Nowadays, the line between the show and the commercial has been blurred: a crate of Target towels is dropped on a deserted beach for the castaways in *Survivor* after which they compete in a reward challenge for Doritos or Mountain Dew. I challenge you to find a current Hollywood movie in which the leading character doesn't sip a cup of Starbuck's coffee.

> Noise is the first thing that gets filtered out.

It seems kind of underhanded, but you can't argue with success. In the 1982 Spielberg film, *ET*, the main character loved Reese's Pieces. Word is that this feature length commercial increased sales of the candy by 65%. They used to give us a story so we would watch the commercials. Now the commercials are embedded into the story.

I Don't Eat Bacon Either

But maybe there never was a line. Most viewers would be surprised to find out how much influence advertisers have always played in determining the actual content of the story. Almost 30 years ago, it was reported that

> *Cereal companies request that programs they buy heavily into do not have characters who eat bacon and eggs for breakfast.*
> Mankiewicz and Swerdlow, *Remote Control*

Wait, there's more.

> *The American Florist Association has successfully kept bereaved characters in television serials from saying that contributions to a charitable organization should be made in lieu of flowers.*
> Mankiewicz and Swerdlow, *Remote Control*

And creepy as that is, and it is creepy, especially for those of us who watched our fair share of TV (I pretty much only watch as research nowadays), if you remind yourself of the business function of all this storytelling, it all makes sense.

TV shows tell stories to sell airtime. Newspapers relate current events to sell ads in print. Movies tell stories to sell popcorn. And you'll tell stories to sell your stuff.

Once you've found your story, you'll have to find a way to connect it with what you're selling and tell it well, all in just 30 seconds.

S C E N E 8

The 30 Second Infomercial

*I*n business, you'll need to write lots of scripts —
speeches, presentations, seminars, but none is more
important than the 30 second "infomercial". Infomercials, elevator pitches, commercials, whatever you call 'em,
you gotta have one — a little show, ready at all times. You
never know when you're going to be called onto the stage.

My Credentials

Before I begin to spout out about infomercials (and there
will be spouting out), let's briefly review my credentials
on this subject. I've watched more than my share of TV
commercials, I've been in them, both on TV and in the
cinema, and I've studied Cannes Award Winning Commercials. (OK, so maybe "studied" is a bit of an exaggeration; I ate cheesecake while watching 'em at a neat little
joint called The Groaning Board in Toronto.) So, if you're
content with my qualifications, let's proceed.

There are two different varieties of infomercials, the
ones you do for a group audience, and the one you perform one-on-one, like when Bill Gates happens to get on

the elevator you're in. This section focuses on the group infomercial; there are significant differences between the two. For the Gates-in-the-Elevator situation, check out Scene 9.

So, you're going to the chamber of commerce networking meeting to spread the word about your business. How do you put your 30 second show together?

You gotta
1. Figure out what you're selling,
2. Observe who your audience is,
3. Dig around for your story,
4. Connect your story to what you're selling and
5. Find a dynamic way of telling it.

"Off the Air"

Miss any of these steps and you'll quickly find yourself "off the air".

Many clients complain to me, "Tsufit, I can't possibly tell them what I do in just 30 seconds".

Let me tell you, if you can't boil it down to 30 seconds, or better yet, to one sentence, you don't know the essence of what you're selling. If you can't say what you do in 30 seconds, you won't be able to say it in 30 minutes either.

> If you can't say what you do in 30 seconds, you won't be able to say it in 30 minutes either.

My suggestion? Go back to Chapter 3 and figure it out before you continue.

First learn the meaning of what you say, and then speak.
Epictetus, Greek Philosopher

Blinks
••••••••••

And consider yourself lucky to have 30 seconds. Advertisers have now introduced a shorter commercial format, 1-3 second radio and TV spots called "Blinks," as a response to viewers tuning out the full 30 second versions. The goal is to make them *impossible* to tune out. A little too Brave-New-Worldish for me, but no doubt they'll be effective.

Bet thirty whole seconds is sounding nice and long right about now. So let's map it out.

1. Open with a dynamic attention grabbing statement. It can be provocative or part of a story. Remember, start in the middle.
2. Present the problem that your product or service addresses.

When you advertise fire extinguishers, open with the fire.
David Ogilvy

3. Tell us how your product or service solves it, or just make the claim and let 'em come ask you more.
4. Do either step 2 or 3 above (or both) in the form of a story.
5. Tell us your name and/or company name, for the first time, two-thirds of the way through the infomercial.
6. Give us one more enticing sentence related to what you said earlier.
7. Repeat your name and then end on an interesting tag line.

So, let's see this in action.

Another mortgage broker came to me seeking help with her infomercial. She told me that her clients were women in their mid-40s seeking debt consolidation. They came to her because they felt they were drowning in debt. We used their frustration and discomfort as a starting point.

"It's 8:40 AM. The alarm didn't go off and you're 10 minutes late for the big boardroom presentation. You rip open a pack of pantyhose and have a tug of war just to bring them up to your knees.

But it says 'One Size Fits All'! One size doesn't fit all. Not with pantyhose and definitely not with mortgages.

I'm Jessica Blow and I'm a Mortgage Consultant. You can pick up a 'One Size Fits All' mortgage at the bank or you can let me shop for you to find the mortgage that fits you perfectly. Jessica Blow. Blow Mortgages. 'Cause one size never fits all."

That takes about 30 seconds. Here's another version.

"Two things in life never seem to fit quite right. Your panty hose and your mortgage. Can't really help you with the panty hose thing, but I can help you make sure that your mortgage doesn't bind. That it's not too tight. That it feels comfortable.

I'm Jessica Blow. I'm a mortgage consultant. Making life more comfortable, one mortgage at a time."

We identified what her clients are looking for, breathing room, and found a visual that will keep them listening long enough to notice her.

Here's another example of "opening with the fire".

"Congratulations. Your marketing efforts have finally paid off. Bill Gates is flying in to meet with you in the boardroom of your corporate head office. Only problem is that your boardroom is your kitchen table. Do you wipe the spaghetti stains off the wall where the kids threw it last night? Or do you call me, Jane Dane, and rent a fully furnished boardroom by the hour and still have enough money left over to pick up a pizza for the kids on the way home?

Jane Dane, Metro Executive Suites."

When my client, the manager of a shared office facility, debuted this 24 second infomercial, 8 out of the 10 women entrepreneurs listening asked for her brochure.

Connect Your Story to What You're Selling

In high school, I kept myself stocked with O'Henry bars by having a part-time job doing telephone market survey research. One of the surveys was intended to find out whether people knew which TV commercial jingle went with which beer. We found that people knew the jingles but often they couldn't tell us which beer each jingle was for.

It's not just about getting noticed. It's about what you want them to do as a result of noticing you.

> *...what marketers have forgotten and need to remember real soon is that marketing is about selling stuff.*
> Sergio Zyman, *The End of Marketing As We Know It*

Sergio Zyman, former chief marketing officer for Coca-Cola, pulled the wildly popular "Mean Joe Greene" commercials off the air because they weren't selling stuff. Having a great infomercial does *not* guarantee you sales. You gotta connect the dots.

Connect the Dots
·······················

An accountant came to me to critique his intros which were quite stale, just a bunch of information you can find in a book. I sensed that he had a good sense of humor just waiting to come out. Boy, did I strike gold. Now, this guy gives me a run for my money when we're both speaking at the same event. I won't even sit beside him, the biggest compliment I can pay a fellow speaker. I don't want to pale in comparison.

But as I told him recently, he mastered lesson one (find and use your humor/put yourself in the story) but he missed lesson two (connect it to what you're selling). He's funny and memorable, which in itself is a very good thing, but if he wants to turn it into money faster, he'll have to use his humor and stories to make a point. He'll have to connect them to his business.

The Anecdotal Yodel
······························

One of my clients grew up in a 600-year-old farmhouse in the Swiss Alps. Cute little blonde kid, braids, the whole bit. She loved to read growing up but it was a long walk down the mountain to the village library. In putting together her story for a 10 minute presentation, I suggested, "Wouldn't it be cute if we could say your favourite book was *Heidi*?" She said, "Tsufit, it was!" What a coincidence. 'Cause that was her name too! But she had never told her story. She had never connected her story to her book production business. We made the connection!

Navigating Rough Waters

Another client, a motivational speaker and business mentor, has a great story. When she first arrived in Canada, in her early 20s, barely speaking English, she was invited to a cottage by a lake with a friend. To make a long scary story short, she got stranded on a little island and decided that if help didn't come soon, she'd swim across the lake for help. Halfway across the lake, she felt she couldn't go on and almost drowned. But she pushed on.

Like that's not enough ("Welcome to Igloo Country") not long afterwards, she had an encounter with a mama bear in the Yukon who hadn't yet had her afternoon snack. Great story. Compelling! And yet, she was trying to sell her mentoring without connecting to her story.

I suggested she leverage her story by using it in her infomercials and by giving speeches and writing articles titled "How to Navigate Rough Waters" or "Survivor!" or "10 Lessons I Learned From an Angry Mama Bear and How to Apply Them to Your Business".

> Everyone has a story. Find yours and connect it to your business.

Everyone has a story. Find yours and connect it to your business. Show your audience why you are the right person to give them what they're looking for.

I love to entertain my audiences with my infomercials and speeches. I even get requests. But since this is a business and not "Comedy Central", I always make sure I connect my story to what

I'm selling. Here's an audience favorite, complete with asides and stage directions.

> *"I have just been named North America's public speaking coach. [Stage Direction: Bow, so audience applauds.] It's a very great honor.*
>
> *Admittedly, the panel of judges was a little teeny weeny bit small, just me and my mom.*
>
> *Nah, who am I kiddin'? She doesn't think I'm that good. Pretty much just me. But it's still a great honor.*
>
> *I'm Tsufit of Follow That Dream!® I coach entrepreneurs and keynote speakers to be spectacular every time they open their mouths in public.*
>
> *Tsufit, for when you're ready to get noticed!"*

My infomercials are a bit "over the top" for many business owners. Remember, this is a public persona that works for me. Go back to Chapter 3 and find the authentic public persona that works for you.

But in case you still doubt the whole "All Business is Show Business" theory, let me tell you that every single one of my infomercials has brought me clients, people whom I met for the first time the day they heard them. They'd also work on TV or in a written ad.

Life Is One Big Infomercial

Don't wait till you arrive at a business function to start worrying about what you're going to say. Be prepared. Have a whole wardrobe of infomercials ready to go. I have a recipe box of 4 × 6 index cards in my desk drawer that I pull out whenever I'm going out to promote.

The best time to write 'em is when you are inspired. In the tradition of the great authors and inventors, I compose many of my masterpieces in the car at red lights, in the bathtub or during my sleep.

And life is my best inspiration. Here's an infomercial that took me less time to write than to say. My third daughter, Riviera, had just come home from school with the wildly exciting news that she had won the public speaking contest at school. This was even more exciting than you can imagine for the reasons you're about to find out. After spending five minutes rejoicing with her, I secured her permission and the permission of her sisters to write the following networking infomercial, which made its debut at a seminar I was giving an hour later.

"Four years ago, my youngest daughter, Aviva, won the public speaking contest in her school. Three years ago, my oldest daughter, Daniela, won the public speaking contest in her school.

Two years ago, my second daughter, Paloma, won the public speaking contest in her school.

And yesterday, my last remaining daughter, Riviera, the shy one, won the public speaking contest in her school.

I'm Tsufit of Follow That Dream!® I'm a public speaking coach.

Now, far be it from me to exploit my daughters' accomplishments for my own personal gain. But I think the facts speak for themselves...

Tsufit. For when you're ready, to get noticed!"

I feel a bit guilty about the insinuation in that last one because my kids definitely deserve 100% of the kudos for their accomplishments. But it does make for a compelling story.

On the Spot

Recently, I attended a business networking event, with my infomercial all planned and they threw us for a loop. They told us to pair up and introduce another person to the crowd. Talk about pressure! Little Miss "I Coach on Infomercials" had to speak without a script. (Reminds me of those dreams where I was in a Math Exam but I hadn't attended the course all year.) We were given one minute to find out about the other person and write an intro. I used my minute wisely, skipping the small talk and jumping straight to the heart of it, what she wanted to be when she was a kid, hobbies and what aspect of her business she wanted to promote that day. Even with the clock ticking, I managed to extract enough color to whip up something clever and hang onto my title.

In show business, performers have to be ready for anything that's thrown at them. With a little practice, you'll be ready when the curtain rises.

Be Provocative

Be a contrarian. It always gets noticed. I've seen competitors have a friendly tussle, playing off each other's infomercials and the result is that we remember both of them better.

When F. W. Woolworth opened his first store, a merchant on the same street tried to fight the new competition. He hung out a big sign: "Doing business in this same spot for over fifty years." The next day

143

Woolworth also put out a sign. It read: "Established a week ago: no old stock."
                    Peter Hay, *The Book of Business Anecdotes*

Must have learned from my friend, Diane.

Why You?
••••••••••••••

And don't forget the "Two Hats Prohibition" from Chapter 3. Choose one thing to focus on per infomercial. The reason that I remember The Groaning Board out of the hundreds of restaurants I've been to in my life is not because of their scrumptious cheesecake or their amazing rice pilaf. The attraction then, and the reason I remember them now, was the screening of the award winning television commercials.

I've had many clients who answered my "Why you?" question with responses like "'Cause we make the best brownies". They'd clearly fail the quiz on Chapter 1, because, as we established, being great at what you do only gets you to ground level, not above.

So, that's how we do it. But what if you can't find your story?

Adopt A Story
•••••••••••••••••••••

Not all the stories you tell have to be your own.

If you're a financial advisor who specializes in helping older people launch businesses after retirement, you could tell the stories of entrepreneurial late bloomers like Julia Child, Mary Kay Ash, Ray Kroc and Colonel Sanders to inspire your audience and attract them to you.

The *Chicken Soup for the Soul*® series grew from Jack Canfield and Mark Victor Hansen telling other people's stories in their speeches. Because their audiences loved the stories so much, the pair collected them into a best selling series.

Or Make Some Up
....

General Motors Europe launched a fabulous series of car commercials for Opel. One of the commercials shows a patient asking her doctor whether her sex change surgery could be reversed after only three days as a woman. Another spot shows a groom carrying his bride over what we think is the threshold, but in fact, he's returning her to her father's house, because he changed his mind after only three days of marriage. This series of commercials illustrates, with humor and creativity, the benefits of getting a "3 Day Test Drive".

• • •

Great stories. One message. Humor. Color. Visuals. That's how it's done.

Whether you tell your story, adopt one or make one up, make sure there's lots of *you* in it. I tell clients: "If that speech could have come out of anyone else's mouth, don't be giving it."

Make it come alive. If you want your show to be on the air and stay there, you can't just be the narrator. You have to be part of the story.

Remember, it *is* a show. Take the time to write yourself a blockbuster script!

> *If that speech could have come out of anyone else's mouth, don't be giving it.*

SCENE 9

The Art of Schmooze

How To Work The Room

If you learn anything from showbiz, learn how to work a room. Entertainers do it naturally. The independent music scene in Toronto has a networking event appropriately called "The Big Schmooze".

The Big Schmooze

There are business networking events everywhere for every purpose, way beyond the chambers of commerce. There are women's networking events, gay networking events, home-based business events, Christian networking events, referral-based networking events and trade association networking events, all with a business focus.

Don't make the mistake of being too discerning at first. Just try them out and see which ones are productive for you and focus on getting good at working the room.

"Don't Talk to Strangers"
••••••••••••••••••••••••••••••••

When my kids were little, like any good mom, I taught them: "Don't talk to strangers". I even bought 'em *The Berenstain Bears Learn About Strangers* book and some videos in case they didn't believe me. But as networking expert, Susan RoAne, points out, this makes sense for little kids, but not for entrepreneurs. Stars need fans. The more fans, the bigger the star.

How are you going to get fans if you refuse to talk to strangers? A star is someone who makes everyone else feel comfortable, someone who'll speak to anyone regardless of how important that person appears or doesn't appear to be.

> I've learned to walk into a room like everyone there is already a friend.

Everyone you haven't met yet is a stranger. I've learned to walk into a room like everyone there is already a friend. I learned this from my years on stage. After a few years of applause, you learn to trust that the audience will like you. So why wait?

I walk into a room like I'm walking on stage.

"Don't Play With Matches" and Other Stuff My Mother Told Me
•••

It's a risky business. They might *not* like me. And my mom did teach me "Don't play with matches" but how else are you gonna light a fire?

Don't be too polite. Rude is no better, but politeness, political correctness, can be a barrier to intimacy, to connection.

That said, I've experienced the opposite. I met a woman who let the details of her trials and tribulations dominate our first five minute encounter and I must admit even I ran for the hills. Too much, too soon. Who asked ya?

Another risk is appearing slimy or sleazy or like you're "on the make". Fan collecting is an art. Fans don't want to feel like they're being collected. They have to feel that they've had a genuine connection with you. So don't be too slick. Just be real and warm and outgoing and your natural charisma will emerge.

You Can't Just Spout Out Your Canned 30 Seconds

I can't tell you how many times, I've been at some kind of business networking event and made the mistake of asking someone what he did for a living. Out comes an overly scripted "selly" corporate sounding infomercial intended for an audience of a hundred people. It's just plain weird being on the receiving end of that, and that's an understatement.

> Fan collecting is an art. Fans don't want to feel like they're being collected. They have to feel that they've had a genuine connection with you.

A recitation of the whole 30 second infomercial you crafted in the last section will sound robotic if you deliver it one-on-one. You don't want to sound like an automaton. Use some of the ideas from your infomercial, but tone it down and leave room for a response from the person to whom you're speaking.

In a one-on-one encounter, the main objective is not to communicate information but rather to connect. The same is true when addressing a crowd, but one-on-one, it's paramount.

The old "Play the Host" principle works well, because many of the people in any given room are nervous and uncomfortable talking to strangers. I go to events I've never been to before and people think I'm running the joint. I make myself right at home and start welcoming others.

The initial connection you make with the people in the room doesn't have to be a business connection, probably better if it isn't. Let people see you as a real person first. It'll strengthen your relationship to the point where it moves naturally into the business arena. That said, my comment at the beginning of this chapter about clients hiring me after a 30 second exposure stands. It happened this morning. And often, like this morning, there was a line-up to speak to me. And I wasn't the speaker! All I had was 30 seconds, the same 30 seconds that everyone else in the room had.

If you've created a strong well defined persona and understand what you have to offer people, it doesn't have to take long.

I've just spent many pages focusing on what to say and how to say it. But if you want a PhD in Schmooze, you'll have to master the fine art of listening.

Be a Sparkling Conversationalist
••

Dale Carnegie used to tell a story of when he attended a society event and was introduced to one of the socialites. She says to him "You're Dale Carnegie. I've heard so much about you." Carnegie responds "And I've heard that you just came back from a trip to Europe". And then, the woman yaps for half an hour about her trip to Europe.

The next day, the society papers quote the woman as saying "I met Dale Carnegie last night. He's a sparkling conversationalist."

Sparking conversationalist? The guy didn't say a word! He just listened. He let *her* be the star. And the result was he got another member in *his* fan club.

There are entire books devoted to the subject of one-on-one business networking (check out RoAne's *How To Work A Room!®*), but here's the bottom line. Focus on attracting and then on making a real connection with those you attract.

Don't come with clipboards to sign people up for a free introductory coaching session. Don't wear your cell phone on a cord around your neck. Just walk in with a big warm smile on your face and be open. Be the best version of you. If you only do one thing to promote your business, go networking and carry yourself like the star that you are.

THE PERFORMANCE

The Script Matters
....

*B*ut get this... Harvard did a study. And I guess they must have run out of rats and aspartame, 'cause this time, they studied people. Turns out *"what* you say" only accounts for 7% of the impression you make on people.

So, let's just get this straight. You learn your trade, you write your script, you throw in some nuns, and it only counts for 7%?

Your delivery is crucial.

SCENE 1

"I'd Like To Thank The Academy"

Presentation Is like Pizza

*M*ost business people focus entirely on content (what they're gonna say) and completely ignore delivery (how they're gonna say it). So the content (the pizza) is great! It's got anchovies, three kinds of cheese, (I'm talking Monterey Jack!), green peppers, pineapple, all the fixin's. But the delivery, that's another matter. Guido, he's the delivery guy, well let's just say he's new. And he really wants to beat the "30 minutes or free" guarantee.

So when he drops the pizza, he just looks both ways, blows all the germs off it (no one saw him sneeze anyway), shoves it back in the box, and he makes it in 28½ minutes. 90 seconds to spare. Go Guido!

What I'm saying is that all the content in the world is not going to make up for a lousy delivery!

The reverse, lousy content with great delivery, sometimes does work. Anyone remember the Spice Girls? They used to say that Richard Burton could read the New York telephone book and make it sound like Shakespeare.

But ultimately, both the content and the delivery need to be dynamic if you want to have staying power. So, how can you rate your own delivery?

Take the TV Test

The square box doesn't lie. The best way to see what you got is to put yourself on TV.

In the film business, they have "dailies", a screening of the footage they got the day before. In live theater, the director gives "Notes". In your business, since you are both the star and the director, you

> *Most business presentations wouldn't last on TV as long as a cowboy on a bull in a rodeo.*

should do what they do in sports, watch the instant replays.

Watch the Instant Replays

Screw up your courage and have yourself videotaped next time you make any kind of a presentation in public. The courage is needed not for the taping, but for the watching. I won't kid you, it can be scary. But you gotta do it anyway.

Would You Stop on This Channel?

Here comes the test part. Sit on the couch, across from the TV, with a remote in your hand. Start channel surfing, then click onto your video, and ask yourself the million dollar question. "Would you stop on this channel?"

Then, ask yourself, if you were already watching it, how long would you *stay* on this channel before you picked up the remote to see what else is on?

Be honest. Most business presentations wouldn't last on TV as long as a cowboy on a bull in a rodeo.

I was thrown into the TV Test when I was only 17. I sang and played guitar with a friend on a TV show that featured undiscovered talent in small towns. Boy, was I shocked when I saw myself on the tube! Thankfully, no tape survives, but the one time I saw it, I witnessed myself looking up at the ceiling when I was singing because I was too shy to look at the audience. The result was that I looked like I had some kind of developmental challenge.

Before you throw the tape into a box in the basement, watch it a second time, but this time stick it on mute. Is it captivating? Check out your facial expressions, your movement.

I often review the tapes of clients with them after their presentations. You can't beat the TV Test for getting to the truth of the matter.

When you stand up, pretend you're on stage. 'Cause you are.

So How Can You Give a Great Performance?

Take the Stage

Before we dig deeper into the nitty gritty of performing, here's a trick that could *literally* be called "positioning". When I go into a room full of business people, I increase my chances of seducing the spotlight by carefully selecting where I place myself in the room.

Never sit in the interior part of the room facing out because your back will always be to half the "audience". If the room is long and narrow choose to sit in the center of the widest wall, facing the whole room with the shortest possible distance between you and every other person in the room, without having your back to anyone. This applies whether you are the keynote speaker or simply in the audience waiting to give your 30 second introduction.

Many times, I've managed to get more attention (and clients) in 30 seconds than the keynote speaker in 30-60 minutes, simply by being well positioned and knowing how to connect with the crowd.

"I'd Like to Thank the Academy"

When you stand up, pretend you're on stage. 'Cause you are. Feel the spotlight shining on you. Move your chair back, a couple of minutes before you have to stand up, so that there's no disturbance when you do.

Bounce like a basketball player. Be agile, ready, in the zone, even if you're nervous. This stance loosens you up.

A Moment of Silence

Pause ... before you speak. Give yourself a second to get their attention. Silence ... can be one of the best attention getters! It gets your audience to look up and listen.

I Got Rhythm!

There's a rhythm and music to speaking in public. There's also choreography.

I'm a singer. I accent the words and phrases and pauses in my clients' infomercials and speeches

Silence... can be one of the best attention getters!

after they're written. Often clients think they can substitute a phrase for a word and make it even better. It doesn't work! Because each comma, each pause is part of the rhythm like in a song. Try substituting a phrase for a word in a song. Doesn't work!

Timing is Everything!

Comedians know this: "Timing is Everything!"

Practice out loud! I change words if my rhythm's wrong. Even if I don't know which word to use at that moment, I stick in a placeholder till I get the rhythm right. When writing infomercials with clients, I might say "We need a two syllable word here". I also help them choreograph the speech or introduction.

> We want "white space" not "dead space". White space creates drama. Dead space creates boredom.

I was watching a client's videotape recently and pointed out to her that the problem was not the speech itself, but rather the pacing. She showed me a 42 minute speech that could have been 30 minutes, tops. There were lulls that she hadn't been aware of while she was on stage.

White Space Not Dead Space

We want "white space" not "dead space". White space creates drama. Dead space creates boredom. A restless audience has one foot out the door.

One way to make sure the pacing is tight, so that the presentation keeps moving and your audience moves with you, is to make sure you know your speech inside and out.

Rehearse, Rehearse, Rehearse

I was recently one of two sources for an article about entrepreneurs' 30 second networking introductions. The journalist said that the other expert and I both recommended that you shouldn't over rehearse, that your bit will lose its spark if memorized. Boy did she get that one wrong!

Rehearse. In the car. In the shower. During sex. Rehearse.

Know Your Lines!

> Rehearse. In the car. In the shower. During sex. Rehearse.

Business people are afraid of sounding over rehearsed. Ain't no such thing!

In show business, no one would even think of jumping on stage and "winging it". Can you imagine a ballerina being told not to over-rehearse? Jerry Seinfeld rehearses every nuance, every inflection. Over and over again. Stars know that the better rehearsed you are, the more spontaneous you sound.

Don't End Up on the Wrong Side of the Tracks

Remember that old Tom Hanks movie, *Bonfire of the Vanities*, where he and Melanie Griffiths take the wrong exit on the highway and end up in a bad neighborhood? Things go from bad to worse. That's happened to me in speeches. One wrong turn and you're lost.

Give special attention to rehearsing the transitions from topic to topic. I tell my clients that if I woke them up at 3 A.M. and gave them a line from their speech, they should be able to tell me the next line or the next topic, automatically, without thinking.

Once I know my speech, I spend extra time rehearsing the transitions. I become like a drill sergeant, till I know them inside out. These are the seams that hold the garment together. These are the reinforced corners in your drywall, the extra gusset in your pantyhose... OK, I can see that you get the point. If you don't know your transitions cold, the whole thing can unravel.

Don't Rehearse It Wrong

As I said, after rehearsals, directors give "Notes", feedback on the performance with suggestions on how to make improvements. There's a reason that plays and movies have directors. Get an objective person, a coach or talented friend, to listen and critique your performance and give you "Notes".

I mentioned that, during my sessions with clients, I often take time to go through and choreograph and accent a speech or infomercial. Clients often tell me, "Don't worry. I just have to practice it." That's what worries me. I don't want them to practice a mistake. Get it right. Then rehearse.

Make a Choice

By now, you already know that you have to distinguish yourself. Be unique. Actors are told, in books about auditioning, to make strong choices for their character. Play the guy gay or with a limp or angry. You might not get the gig but at least you'll be remembered and who knows, they may just change the role. Make an impression! The same thing applies to building your business persona and writing and performing your infomercials. Don't sit on the fence. Take a stand. Make a choice.

Make It Your Own

There also has to be lots of "you" in it.

Singers are told this all the time. Very few singers ever get famous by singing "cover tunes", songs made famous by someone else. And those who do (Whitney Houston singing Dolly Parton's "I Will Always Love You", Elvis singing Carl Perkins' "Blue Suede Shoes"), make it their own. They bring originality to it, a new point of view.

That's what entrepreneurs have to do when they market something that can be bought anywhere from anyone; they have to make it their own. They have to have a unique point of view.

Better Bad Than Boring!

I was reading a book by a casting director who said that it's better to be bad than boring. She's right. At least you'll be remembered. No one buys boring.

Be yourself, only bigger!

Kick it up a notch. So people can see it.

Take a Risk!

It's all over in 30 seconds anyway!

Take a Risk! It's all over in 30 seconds anyway!

Accent It!
••••••••••••••

If you have an accent, don't try to hide it. Embrace it! An accent didn't hurt Dr. Ruth or Governor — what's his name?... Schwarzenegger.

Keep It Fresh
••••••••••••••••••••

The secret of putting on a fantastic show is keeping it fresh. Unexpected. Madonna is a master at this.

But the new experiences you give your audience still have to be consistent with your established persona. Your brand can evolve — note Cher's odyssey from camp pop star clothes-horse to Academy Award winning actress (and some might argue back again), but expect some audience resistance if you move too quickly. You may have a "New Coke" type revolution on your hands. The trick is to keep the audience engaged while still fulfilling their expectations.

Use Props, But Go Easy on the Boas!
••

As you already know, I never go anywhere without broccoli. And audiences love when I pull a Pepsi Can out of the oversized Coke tin I picked up at Value Village for $2.99.

Remember "Show and Tell" from when we were kids? Which one got top billing? I rest my case.

Actually, wait. I take that back. You can go too far with the props. Don't let them become a distraction. You don't want to look like a magician whose bunny refuses to pop out on cue. Me, personally, I've seen one too many boas on stage. Just use props to flavor your presentation. Don't drown yourself out.

Know Your Audience

··························

Knowing your audience starts long before the performance on stage. It starts with the launch of your business
and with every script you write.

But when you're going to open your mouth in public,
you'll also want to know something about the people who'll
be witnessing you do it. Whenever possible, I try to go see
a show in the venue I'll be performing or speaking in, just
to check it out. How is the seating arranged? What kind
of people show up? How are they dressed? What do they
laugh at?

I used to do the same thing when I was a lawyer. If I
had to appear in a court I'd never been in, I'd go check it
out ahead of time.

A producer was just telling me the other day about a
comedienne who used blue humor for a group of busi-
nessmen who didn't even crack a smile.

Margaret Cho tells a story about being booked as the
entertainment for — well, I'll let her tell it:

> *I did a gig last Saturday night, not something that*
> *unusual but it was not my typical show. It was a*
> *corporate convention, the kind I normally avoid...*
> *After about 10 mins. my mic was turned off and the*
> *band...was hurried on to the stage. They passed me*
> *looking apologetic...as they launched in to a rousing*
> *rendition of 'Sweet Home Alabama'.*
>
> *www.margaretcho.com*

Knowing your audience doesn't mean pandering to
them or changing who you are, but it does mean being
sensitive in your presentation. I used to speak to judges
differently than I speak to audiences now. Setting aside

the fact that the judges had the power to throw me in the slammer for contempt if I was out of line, or kick me out of the courtroom if I wasn't dressed properly, any audience can give you the pink slip if you're not connecting.

Audiences can tune in or tune out while they wait for the next act. How often do you listen to the local politician's opening remarks when you came to hear the keynote speaker? Good time for a last minute washroom break unless he really grabs you.

Your Audience Doesn't Have the Script

Don't worry so much about remembering what you plan to say that you forget to connect with your audience. Remember, your audience doesn't have the script. But we do know if you are talking *to* us or talking *at* us. Some of my best moments on stage were when I forgot my lines.

I was right between verse three and verse four of the song, "Gold Watch Blues", when my mind went on vacation. I had no clue how to start the next verse. But because I was really there with my audience, I was able to come up with a diversion (I had them do a rattle solo — you had to be there!) which turned out to be even funnier than the verse I had forgotten.

If I had become self-conscious about forgetting my lines, I would have been toast. Have you ever been in a comedy club when the comedian was nervous or forgot his lines? You're dying for him. It makes the audience nervous too.

Once a performer loses control of the audience, he's done. It's very hard to win 'em back. A performer needs to make an audience feel taken care of. Like he's got it all under control.

The Comeback — Don't Leave Home Without It
....

Johnny Carson was better known for his comebacks on jokes that didn't work than for the jokes themselves. You'll stay in the spotlight only as long as you connect with your audience.

Carson was also a master of the art of reaction, as was Jack Benny. Carson always had excellent comebacks in his pocket. Matthew Perry, from *Friends*, like Benny, can do it with just a look or a sigh.

I always have a few stock reactions ready for emergencies, like when an audience member upstages me with a joke to top my joke. I let 'em have their laugh and when it dies down I throw out the standard "Thanks. I work alone." Never fails to get a laugh. (I wish I had remembered to do that when my then 6-year-old daughter yelled out the punch line to my comedic song in front of an audience of 1400 people.) Jerry Seinfeld has a great line to deal with people who yell out from the crowd. "Thanks, I'll take it from here..."

Just like when you're working a room, I tell clients to walk up to the podium imagining that the people in the room, the members of the audience, are all friends. They already like you. So, you don't have to work to win them over. It's amazing how well that works!

Deleted Scenes
....

Did I mention that "less is more"? Bears repeating. Recently, my kids and I watched deleted scenes from *The Notebook* which we'd seen on DVD the night before. ("Five thumbs up" by the way, Rachel McAdams and Ryan Gosling tear up the screen.) It occurred to me afterwards how much better the movie was without those scenes even though the scenes helped explain the story a little more.

There's a reason that film directors and authors rely on outside editors to shape their work — sometimes you just need an outside pair of eyes, a fresh discerning take on your work. And there's a reason they give Academy Awards for Best Editor. Editors are like sculptors. It's what they take away that gives the art its shape.

Less Is More

If you're the keynote speaker and you're offered an hour to speak, tell them you only need 30 to 45 minutes and be prepared to take questions. Less is definitely more! On several occasions I've seen a speaker wow an audience in the first 45 minutes, only to bore them to tears for another hour after that.

My kids help me edit my speeches. And they can be tough. Whenever they suggest I cut something, I greet their suggestion with the same enthusiasm as when someone "suggests" I throw out the Pinocchio marionette who lost his head years ago. I fight for my poor vulnerable paragraph and force them to wrestle me to the ground. But they're usually right.

Director's Cut

Get yourself a great "editor" or at least make a very discerning "Director's Cut" of your own work. Who even knows if this paragraph will survive...

Don't Sell From the Stage

I've been listening to a series of teleseminars and they couldn't be more different. Some are truly informative and others are 90 minute commercials for the speaker.

It's one thing to inform us for 85 minutes and then mention your stuff at the end. But be warned. Even that can put off an audience. All of a sudden, your responsive audience raises its guard and you leave them with a sour taste in the mouth.

It flabbergasts me (now there's a word!) how many accomplished speakers will jeopardize their credibility for a few sales.

Audiences are pretty much unanimous on this one. I recently saw people walking out on the presentation of a guy who really knew his stuff when he got to the "Pay Me Money" portion of the show.

This is not a "bird in the hand is worth two in the bush" situation. Because the two in the bush have friends. If the one in the hand feels caught, he won't tell anyone, or worse yet, he'll tell them all to avoid you.

Attract, don't chase!

Never Open With New Material
....

In Seinfeld's documentary, *Comedian*, he and other comedy veterans discuss the dangers of breaking the "Never open with new material" rule. It's tempting but resist. Open with something that's worked before, establish yourself with the audience as being in control and only then take the risk of incorporating a new bit. Violate this principle at your peril.

Open Off Broadway
....

Do like they do in show business. I've said it before. Open off Broadway.

Test your speeches, and just about everything else, where it doesn't really count. I used to go try out songs

I'd just written at an underground café that has produced several of North America's top folk and pop artists. We'd test our stuff in front of a very forgiving audience of other musicians, just to see the reaction. I always went there before a big show. Seinfeld spent a year developing an entirely new act after leaving his hit TV show. He parked his ego at the door and went from comedy club to comedy club doing short sets, trying new bits, taking 6 full months to work up to a measly half hour of solid new material! He spent several more months to beef it up to an hour. So don't be hard on yourself if it takes a while to perfect your script or your performance.

Be Your Own Warm Up Act

Stars know they have to start strong and finish with confidence. I've had speakers tell me, "It takes a while for me to get going but by the end, I'm warmed up and going strong". That's too late. Your audience will turn the channel on you long before you get a chance to warm up.

That's why they have "warm up" acts for concerts and comedy acts and TV shows that are taped live. By the time the star hits the stage, the audience is warmed up and ready to be receptive. In your business life, most of the time, you'll have to be your own warm up act.

"Never Look Straight into the Camera" and Other Rules Meant to Be Broken

It's customary, at large networking events, to stand up when you deliver your 30 second elevator pitch to the audience. Rules are made to be broken.

I once started delivering my 30 second business info-mercial sitting down, so that 80 business types had to crane their necks to see me. When I finally stood up in the middle of the infomercial (which was on the subject of how to attract attention to your business) all eyes were on me in a way I've never experienced before. It was as if the mere act of standing up became an event, just because I did it at an unexpected time, to punctuate what I was saying.

The Art of the "Aside" or Breaking the Fourth Wall
••••••••••••••••••••

Many performers use the TV camera as a second audience. Johnny Carson would talk to his studio audience and then aim a comment or even a look, a wink or a shrug, directly at the camera.

I use a similar device when I'm speaking in front of a live audience. I interrupt myself to say something directly to my audience. In theater, this is called "breaking the fourth wall", acknowledging, in the middle of a play, that there is an audience and speaking directly to them. It makes a huge impact.

When speaking to an audience, for a moment, I'll leave the scripted presentation behind, change my tone of voice to an even more conversational, conspiratorial, "by the way" kind of voice, and tell 'em something "off the record", as if I just thought of it on the spur of the moment. Ninety-nine times out of a hundred that "spur of the moment" interruption is well rehearsed.

It usually takes me more than three weeks to prepare a good impromptu speech.

Mark Twain

Arthur Laurents described Barbra Streisand's Marmelstein audition as "calculated spontaneity".

If you master the art of the aside, you'll notice your audience perk up, physically raise their eyes to you in a whole new way, as if you are about to tell them a secret. Sometimes, regardless of how good a speaker you are, the audience filters out the main voice, the narrator, but it will never miss an aside.

Should You Ad Lib?

Hamlet says "Speak no more than is set down". Old Willie knew what he was talking about. Stick to the script, stuff that you know works. But like all good rules, you can break this one occasionally. Just exercise caution.

You're On

Don't wait till your foot hits the stage to be in character.

The audition really starts in the waiting room.
Messaline and Newhouse, *The Actor's Survival Kit*

It often surprises me that entrepreneurs attending networking functions don't understand that the networking starts the minute you open the car door. I once said "hi" to a woman in the parking lot, only to be ignored till we were introduced at the function itself. Maybe she didn't know that I was going to the same event she was. So what? I've hired people I've met in the ladies' washroom.

Staying in Character

Similarly, some speakers are your best friend when they're on stage and then cool and aloof one-on-one. Maybe they're shy. More on that below. But it's a good way to lose your audience. Maybe some of you don't attend business networking functions. But even if you're just out and about, it pays to be warm and it pays to be entertaining. All the world's a stage. And the entertaining shall inherit the earth.

Ta Da!
••••••••••

My two younger daughters, Riviera and Aviva, took gymnastics for a couple of years. The first thing they taught 'em, before the balance beam, before the cartwheel — was how to present at the end of the move. Like at the Olympics. Have you seen Olympic skaters? No matter how many times they fall on the ice, the ending is always spectacular! They hold their arms out in the air.

Ta Da! Like a star!

> All the world's a stage. And the entertaining shall inherit the earth.

SCENE 2

Don't Be Shy!

But What If I'm Shy?
....

*L*ike many performers when you catch them off the stage, Johnny Carson was, according to many who knew him well, shy. Painfully shy. And yet, there are also many accounts of people feeling intimidated by him.

The shy man does have some slight revenge upon society for the torture it inflicts upon him. He is able, to a certain extent, to communicate his misery. He frightens other people as much as they frighten him.
                                        Jerome K. Jerome, Author

I'm shy. (Except when I'm not.) I remember when I was a kid, having my mom call me to come into the living room to meet her friends. I refused. I was too shy.

When I was in my 20s, I was spending a summer in my hometown and performing at a local outdoor café. I'd sit there and sing my pretty little songs, till one day, one of my mom's friends came up to me after the show and said, "Tsufit, get your face out of the guitar and talk to the audience!" I did and next thing you know I'm doing standup comedy on national TV.

So, what if you're shy?

Get Over It!
• • • • • • • • • • • • • • • •

OK. That was harsh. But true, nonetheless. The way to get over it is to realize that shyness is just discomfort with the situation you're in.

Stage Fright
• • • • • • • • • • • • • • • •

If you have stage fright, first of all, know that you're not alone. Even in show business, where, by definition, the whole business exists for the purpose of putting on shows, stage fright is rampant. Even the most famous performers, people like Barbra Streisand and Carly Simon, admit to suffering from it.

There's stage fright and there's stage fright. One kind is the pounding you get in your chest before you step onto the stage. That's normal and often doesn't go away till you're up there and connecting with the people. Don't let it stop you from stepping onto the stage.

> *It's natural to have butterflies. The secret is to get them to fly in formation.*
> Walter Cronkite

The other kind of stage fright, the dry mouth, "can't breathe" kind, can be a problem. It happens to most of us once in a while, usually when we're intimidated by our audience. I remember singing a song I hadn't quite perfected to a panel of radio programmers for critique and was surprised that the pounding in my chest never really went away. That's why people give the "picture them in their underwear" advice, so you won't be intimidated.

I think the answer has nothing to do with underwear. The answer is to always speak in your own voice. It's about connecting with your audience.

> I think the answer has nothing to do with underwear. The answer is to always speak in your own voice.

Sincerity: If you can fake it, you've got it made.
Daniel Schorr, Journalist

Change the Setting

When I was in grade nine, my dad took a sabbatical in Illinois, which meant that I had to spend the last year of Junior High in a new school. In Biology class, the tables were arranged in a big hollowed out square and everyone faced everyone and it was very comfortable. Every morning at 9 A.M., I was the Tsufit I am today — funny, confident, engaging and modest.

But every afternoon, in French class, I was a mouse. Shy, nervous, uncomfortable. The desks were arranged in traditional row style and I was behind, since in Canada we had not yet learned written French. I got Ds on my first few tests.

Same person, same school, many of the same kids in both classes, but every day, two different personalities. I later felt the same discomfort in law firms.

It's my experience that labeling yourself "shy" is inaccurate and misleading. If you change the setting to a situation you're comfortable in, you'll be surprised to find your shyness fall away. (More on that in Chapter 7.)

One more showbiz trick to overcome the shyness. Step into character.

I can sing in front of 1500 people in an amphitheater, but ask me to pull out a guitar and entertain eight friends at a party and I won't do it. It happened recently. Girls weekend at a friend's cottage. She asked me to sing for the gang. "Oops, I forgot my guitar." Like many performers, I need some distance between me and the audience. When I walk on stage, I step into my character and then it's not me that's vulnerable up there, it's "Performer Barbie". Of course, I'm still me and of course, I still connect, but it's the distance that helps you overcome the feeling of being naked up there.

> It's my experience that labeling yourself "shy" is inaccurate and misleading. If you change the setting to a situation you're comfortable in, you'll be surprised to find your shyness fall away.

Speaking of Public Speaking...

It's the weirdest thing. Stick a really fun charismatic person behind a podium and all of a sudden he's giving the Gettysburg Address.

Why do we need courses in Public Speaking? You know how to speak. You've been doing it since you were two, just like walking. It's not like you have to take a course in Public Walking.

Like I said earlier, we have to *unlearn* a bunch of stuff we learned at Corporate School. Just be yourself.

Easier said than done.

The best way to conquer stage fright is to know what you're talking about.

Michael Mescon, Author

Great quote and it definitely helps if you know your stuff, but I'm not sure that's the whole story. Many experts get tongue tied in public.

Although "being yourself" should be a snap..., it's the toughest acting job you'll ever have to do. The situation is tense and unnatural. If you were really being yourself, you would plead for the job or babble on about how nervous you are or embarrass yourself in a dozen other socially unacceptable ways.

Messaline and Newhouse,
The Actor's Survival Kit

> We have to unlearn a bunch of stuff we learned at Corporate School. Just be yourself.

I've had success with self-proclaimed "shy" people by just helping them make themselves more comfortable in the situation they're in, by bringing more of themselves to the situation and by coaching them to go back to speaking naturally, in their own voice, instead of the way they think they're supposed to speak. Speaking the way we think we're supposed to doesn't feel natural or comfortable.

You don't have to sound polished or professional to be a star. We forget how to just talk to people. That's what giving a presentation is. Talking to people.

All that Glitters is Not Gold
••••••••••••••••••••••••••••••••••••

I was at a conference, recently, where I observed two very different people in the spotlight. One was a modest best-selling author and the other was a gorgeous glitzy singer. The singer was all "razzle dazzle 'em", beautiful, sparkly, confident with a powerful singing voice, all good things. And yet, in speaking to several audience members afterwards, I found that my impression was shared by others. She hadn't connected. We didn't care about her or what she was saying. It was empty glitter.

The humble author, on the other hand, told a few heart felt stories and then walked out to a long line-up of fans, many of whom bought multiple copies of his book for autographing.

The author spoke in his own voice. He wasn't speaking to impress or sound professional. He was sincere. In fact, this record breaking best-selling author hadn't even written his book seeking fame; he wrote it for his two young daughters.

Don't be shy!

Be Your Own Stage Manager

Let's Get Technical
....

*N*o matter how big you get, and how many employees you hire, in many ways, your business really is a one man show. And you're in charge. People as big as Oprah advise "Always sign your own checks". You're the Executive Producer.

You're not only the Director, Producer and Star, you're also the Stage Manager. So you're gonna have to know your way around the theater.

Unlike the red carpet scene you see at the Academy Awards, you probably won't be arriving in a limo, and no chauffeur named Henri will be carrying your bags. You won't be arriving at the last second after the audience is seated like at a movie premiere, you'll be arriving two hours ahead of time, if you're smart, to case out the joint.

I arrive before the organizer arrives so I can move chairs and tables around to best showcase me. (Oh, the glamour of being a star!) By the time the person in charge arrives, she usually thinks that's the way the venue set it up. I befriend the staff at the location and they'll usually do anything for me when I need them; they're usually relieved not to have to deal with another diva.

For a 50-minute keynote, I bring enough luggage for a two week cruise. I always bring a change of clothing (you never really know how to dress till you see the place), some props, some index cards for audience comments, but most importantly I bring the essentials below.

BYOP (Bring Your Own Podium)

I was asked, with short notice, to fill in as MC for a fundraising event at a theater. Till that point in my career, I just stood behind whatever podium I was given. On my acting resume, I claim to be 5'4" tall, but that's standing on a suitcase, and sometimes the lectern is taller than I am. The star of that evening was a popular national radio show host, and I was asked to do my five minutes of hilarity and then introduce him, all from the elephant podium at the side. Remembering my "Always Take Center Stage" rule, I quickly informed the crew that I'd do it without the podium. I noticed a lone music stand on the stage and decided it'd do the trick.

It was fantastic, so I bought my own. Now I don't leave home without it. It's portable. It's adjustable. Nothing blocking me. I can stand to the left of it and speak to my audiences with no barrier, like mother nature intended. I send all my speaking clients out to buy them.

Microphones

Where possible, I don't use them. While I would never sing without the beautiful reverb I get on my vocal mic, I avoid speaking with microphones unless I'm in a particularly large venue.

Unless you bring your own system (expensive, cumbersome, some may say overkill), you'll generally be given a crappy "Don't-worry-it's-great-we-use-it-for-all-our-functions" house microphone that thins and distorts your voice and makes you sound like you are 10 miles away or in a cave. And it ties you down. Even a cordless hand-held microphone occupies one of your hands that has better things to do. If there's no choice, agree to a lapel mic, but don't be pounding your chest to emphasize your points. Or buy yourself one of those "I-freelance-as-a-telephone-operator-on-weekends" wireless headset microphones with a small portable receiver. And don't forget to turn the microphone off when you go to the washroom!

Author's Note: I wrote that last line months ago, but I had to stop everything to add this, if only for the "told 'ya so" factor. Breaking news — CNN Award-winning news anchor leaves her microphone on and is caught yapping in the washroom with her friend. The whole thing gets broadcast over the President's live address to the nation! My work is never done...

Bring Backup

When I was performing in an episode of a comedy show that was to be taped in front of a live audience and broadcast on national TV, I inquired repeatedly whether they'd have the proper sound system to accommodate a music track I was planning to sing to. "Of course" they would. I threw a boom box into the van, just in case.

Close call. They had nothing!

When I'm setting up at a venue, the first guy I look for is the sound guy. Make him your new best friend. He can make or break you. Lights are important too.

Don't Upstage Yourself
••••••••••••••••••••••••••••••••

The best way to keep on top of things when you present is to keep your performances low tech. I realize that what I'm about to say is heresy to the corporate born and bred, but I'll say it anyway — don't use PowerPoint. It's ironic, but PowerPoint actually dilutes your power. Don't rely on any kind of technical devices. Even if they do run smoothly (and what are the chances of that?), they divide the audience's attention between you and the screen. Don't give out handouts. Same reason. You want all eyes on you. Why upstage yourself?

Don't Be Cueless!
••••••••••••••••••••••••••••

Ever catch the TV talk show hosts reading off teleprompters? You probably don't have one and if you heed my advice above, you won't have PowerPoint either. So what *do* you do?

I heard a big time literary agent, on stage, swear by the notes she scribbles in pen all over her hands. I winced when I heard her share this because she was wearing a stunning white suit at the time. She confided that she had indeed once wiped her sweaty palms down the length of her skirt while speaking on stage. My eldest daughter, Daniela, is also a fan of the "pen on the hands" method (much to my chagrin as the one who does the laundry), but I think we're looking for something a little more sophisticated here.

> It's ironic, but PowerPoint actually dilutes your power. Why upstage yourself?

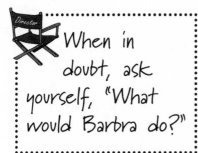

When in doubt, ask yourself, "What would Barbra do?"

Can't get any more sophisticated than the old fashioned 4 × 6 index cards on my music stand. I move 'em every once in a while without taking my eyes off the audience.

Having it all on paper can be risky. Contrast Alan Arkin's 2007 Oscar acceptance speech with Forest Whitaker's the same year. Both read, but Arkin was lost in the paper while Whitaker's was moving in spite of it. If you can't be trusted with the whole story on those cards, and you know who you are, then give yourself a few words or pictures with arrows, anything that will help you know what you're talking about.

Personally, I find it useful to have everything there as an emergency backup, "blank insurance", with the main topics bolded and highlighted. (Bet a certain Miss in South Carolina's gonna stash a few cue cards next time she's at the mic.) I pretty much do the whole thing from memory with a few glances at the headings on the cards.

There are wonderful books out there on different ways to keep on track, but it's best to just experiment and see how you feel most comfortable. Never forget that, even if you're the only one talking, it *is* a conversation.

What Would Barbra Do?

If you think I'm overdoing it on the technicalities of being a star, think again. When in doubt, ask yourself, "What would Barbra do?"

I was a keynote speaker at an event recently. I felt a little embarrassed, but I asked the video guy anyway whether he put a fresh battery in my mic's battery pack. The next evening I saw the part in Seinfeld's documentary where he's checking out the stage for his *Tonight Show* appearance. You know what he said to the sound guy? "Fresh battery?"

Where would J. Lo have been without the duct tape that held her Oscar dress in place? She would have pulled a Janet Jackson.

The biggest stars concern themselves with the details of being a star. When Barbra Streisand finished up her song on Oprah a few years ago, a surprised Oprah said, "I've owned this studio for 15 years and I've never seen a white microphone". Barbra explained that she had the microphone spray-painted white so that it would match her sweater and her dog! She didn't want it to detract from her performance.

If you want to be a star, you're going to do everything possible to set yourself up for stardom. But know, that despite all your careful preparation, you can't control everything. (Believe me, I've tried!)

THE SHOW MUST GO ON!

*T*rue Story. There I am, feeling like quite the starlet in my black and gold sequin dress, singing and dancing on stage, just me and the male lead, when all of a sudden, my skirt drops about eight inches from my waist to my thighs, in front of hundreds of people. I yank it up without missing a beat and keep on dancing.

When the Going Gets Tough, The Tough Get Chocolate
....

At some point, something will go wrong. Not sure if it's the law of averages or the law of Murphy, but I can tell you that expecting it makes it easier when it happens. Here are a few tips for when it gets tough.

A Friend in Need is a Friend Indeed or How the Rabbi's Wife Saved My Life
....

Another reason to arrive early is to scope out the audience as the people arrive. You're looking for potential allies.

When my CD came out, I was invited to sing at a women's event in my home town. As you know, the home town crowd can be tough, even for a seasoned performer. After all, they saw you in diapers. So, I start the show, performing to a group of women my mom's age who knew me as a kid, women who were probably thinking, "Why are we paying to hear her sing? You should hear my son, Bernie, play the violin!"

Tough Room!
....

Only one woman, the Rabbi's wife who had just moved there from New York City, was beaming at me, laughing at every joke, singing along. So I played to her. I did my show just for her. And slowly, slowly, the rest of them came around. Laughter is contagious. By halfway into it, I had the whole audience in the palm of my hand.

If you can't find even one fan in the audience, it's gonna be tough. Work the room before you get on stage to make sure you have at least one or two audience members in your pocket and watch the rest of them follow.

Never Apologize!
....

(A corollary of "Never Let Them See You Sweat".)

If you have a fever of 102 and a nose plugged up from here to Cleveland, ignore it. If you apologize in advance, you are setting the stage for a sub-standard performance, whatever you give them. If you can't manage to be "on" for fifteen minutes at the most, stay home.
Messaline and Newhouse, *The Actor's Survival Kit*

Use It

....

Actors are always being told to "use it in the performance" when something upsetting or challenging happens
in their personal lives. In business, as in show business,
the show must go on.

Several times, I've had to go on stage sick, hard when
you're a singer. But you can't call in sick when you *are* the
show, so I "used it", summoning up a little humor to smooth
out the rough spots and set the stage as best I could.

After telling the audience not to feel sorry for me just
because I had a touch of a cold, I pulled out a box of
Kleenex, then another and another, till I had neatly stacked
a tower of five boxes. I then slowly and deliberately pulled
out a jar of honey, a box of tea, some cough drops, a bottle
of water, some Echinacea and then, while the audience
chuckled, I pulled out my guitar and started the show.

As long as the performer is in control of the show, the
audience will be comfortable.

Does All this Seem Too Hard?

....

Stay home and eat Twinkies! But you gotta ask yourself,
do I really want to be 59 and still making cold calls?

All the great speakers were bad speakers at first.
Ralph Waldo Emerson

Not sure if Waldo's right about that, but I have seen
unbelievable transformations, people dragged out of the
shadows and into the spotlight who now are excited to
jump back in and do it again.

Speaking of the Governor, Arnold Schwarzenegger
knows what it takes to prepare to step into the spotlight.

It's said that the man worked at speaking in public with the same discipline he brought to body building. And he did it in a language foreign to him. If he can do it, so can you.

Every time you have to speak, you are auditioning for leadership.

James Humes

Casting Call
....

If after reading this book from cover to cover, your presentations are about as interesting as watching paint dry, hire a coach to help you or have a casting call. Just because you're the director, doesn't mean you always have to play the lead.

Audition people, either from your organization (maybe you have an extra kid lying around) or from the outside to speak on your behalf. Better if it's you, but if you feel you're not ready yet, find the most energetic charming passionate person you can and make him or her your spokesperson. Jello has Bill Cosby. Nike, McDonald's and Wheaties have Michael Jordan.

You probably can't afford a celebrity, but perhaps you can create one. Keep reading.

CHAPTER 5

"Extra, Extra, Read All About It!"

or

How To Get Your Face in the Newspaper Without Robbing a Bank!

THE POWER OF PUBLICITY

*I*f a tree falls in the forest and no one is there to hear it, does it make a sound?

I figured this one out early on. I asked myself: "If I shlep all the way to Ottawa to sing in a coffee house for 14 people, do I make a sound?"

I contacted the *The Ottawa Sun*. They did a feature article on me with a great color photo. The whole city knew I was coming. I made a sound.

If a tree falls in the forest and no one is there to hear it, does it make a sound?

HERE'S THE SCOOP, THE WHOLE SCOOP AND NOTHING BUT THE SCOOP

We said it in Chapter 1: An "expert" is not someone who knows what he knows. An expert is someone who is *known* for knowing what he knows. In business, as in show business, there's no point in doing what you do if no one knows about it. You gotta get the word out. And one of the best ways to do that is through publicity.

But the tricky thing about publicity is that while it can hugely enhance star status, it doesn't usually create it. The catch is that the media are usually only interested in people who already have an interesting story. That's why you can't present yourself in black and white, like in a child's coloring book. You have to pick up a crayon or two and color yourself in!

Fame
....

Remember that line in the movie, *Fame*, where choreographer, Debbie Allen, says "You got big dreams? You want fame? Well fame costs. And right here's where you start paying, in sweat!"

Welcome Backstage
••••••••••••••••••••••••

Most of us only see a production from the audience's point of view and everything looks pretty glamorous on stage. But have you ever been *in* a show? ("Third Tree to the Left" counts.) Behind the scenes, there are nails to be hammered, sets to be built, backdrops to be painted and costumes to be repaired. All so you can glide onto the stage and make it look effortless. It's the same with publicity.

> *"You got big dreams? You want fame? Well fame costs. And right here's where you start paying, in sweat!"*
>
> Director

Getting publicity is very exciting. Reading about the nuts and bolts of *how* to get publicity? Not so much.

Is it worth it? When asked the secret of the Beatles' success, Ringo Starr replied "We have a press agent." Getting publicity *is* worth the effort it takes to get it. But only if you're ready.

Are You Ready?
••••••••••••••••••••

You'll hear me say this again and again. Publicity is only valuable when you have all your ducks in a row. If yours are still frolicking around the barnyard (where do I get this stuff?), go back and work through Chapters 3 and 4. It'll pay off, big time, in the long run.

This chapter is a "behind the scenes" look at achieving stardom. It's not glamorous but if you're ready to kick your business into high gear, this is the chapter that'll help you do it. OK, enough with the warnings.

Remember, *all* business is show business. A movie studio wouldn't think of operating without a Publicity Department and neither should you.

> Remember, all business is show business. A movie studio wouldn't think of operating without a Publicity Department and neither should you.

You'll need Media Lists, Bios, Photos, Press Releases and a system for keeping track of it all. Most importantly, you'll need a strategy. But, first things first.

Get Organized!

I keep a tattered *Redbook* "Get Organized" Magazine from 1994 in the drawer of my night table and sneak longing glances at it, the way some men look at *Playboy*. I'm talking lust. I crave organization. But sadly, with four kids, it often eludes me.

So I collect organization books. I've got at least 20 or 30. Now, if I could only find them... Cheesy jokes aside, the one area I make the biggest effort to organize is my own personal Publicity Department, 'cause if I can't find a Press Kit when Oprah calls, there goes my big break.

There are many fabulous "how to" publicity books that give you the down and dirty details of how to put together a publicity campaign, how to assemble your press kit, how to write the press release — we won't go into that here. (You can find a list of these books at *www.yourpublicitydepartment.com*.) We're gonna focus on the big picture, how you can *attract* the media and use publicity to enhance your star status.

Just one last thing. If you're not sure about publicity, there is another choice.

Why Not Just Buy an Ad?
....

Pretty much the first thing a new entrepreneur does, after getting some fancy business cards and fancier letterhead, is stick an advertisement in the paper to tell the world: "I'm in business". Ads are easy. You pay your money — they print your ad. But before you put your feet up on your desk and wait for the clients to beat a path to your door, consider what an ad means.

An ad tells the reader that you paid someone money to say that your stuff is good. Or more accurately, that you paid someone money to print the good stuff *you* say about yourself and your business.

On the other hand, an article in a newspaper or magazine makes an editorial comment. It implies that an objective third party, who has no stake in your business, thinks your product or service is good or interesting or worth checking out. Editorial coverage inherently has much more credibility than advertising. Even though he made his living as an "Advertising Man", David Ogilvy recognized this fact.

> *...if you make them [advertisements] look like editorial pages, you will attract about 50 per cent more readers.*
>
> David Ogilvy

A business needs visibility and credibility. Advertising gives you one. Publicity can give you both.

The Power of the Press

Giving them even more clout is the fact that articles are often physically much bigger than any advertising most of us can afford. I was lucky enough to have my photo on the front page of a local newspaper, the whole front page, with only a little Volvo ad underneath. The story itself was given another half page on page three. Volvo shelled out big bucks for a couple of inches under my feet on page one, but it didn't cost me a cent.

Of course, there are expenses related to promoting yourself to the media, but they're negligible compared to the benefit of a good sized feature article with a photo.

Does It Make Sense to Advertise?

Ads can work, in the right circumstances; otherwise, billions of dollars wouldn't be spent on advertising. If you have the budget of Coca-Cola, go ahead. Knock yourself out. But Anita Roddick wouldn't have been able to build The Body Shop on advertising alone. You need to create a buzz, have people talking about you. That's more likely to get started from an editorial comment than from advertising. Publicity, combined with the word-of-mouth it can generate, is the best of all possible worlds.

A business needs visibility and credibility. Advertising gives you one. Publicity can give you both.

So why do so many entrepreneurs shell out the big bucks for three inches of fame?

Lots of reasons. One of the drawbacks of publicity is that you have relatively little control over it. If you plunk down money for an ad, you'll get your name in print just the way you want it. With publicity, it ain't necessarily so. You can send out press releases, be interviewed, even be promised an article and still come up empty handed. If there's a time line involved and you need some ink now, an ad is the sure way to go.

But the main reason most entrepreneurs pay for advertising is because they don't know how else to attract the spotlight. I met a guy a while ago who was complaining that he couldn't get the newspapers to write about his new business. Even his friend, a journalist for the local daily paper, couldn't help. "If I write about you, I have to write about every new business" his friend told him.

The Simple Scoop
....

But don't get discouraged if it seems that the media has all the power. They need us as much as we need them. OK, so that's a lie. We need them more. But, if they have nothing to write about, no one feeding them interesting stories, what are they going to put between ads?

A newspaper or magazine is a business. The higher the circulation, the more they can charge for the ads. So the stories really have to attract readers.

You have to put yourself in the shoes of the editor who's thinking about the guy ultimately reading the paper over eggs and toast. The eggs-and-toast guy wants a good story. The editor wants the eggs-and-toast guy to buy more papers. If your story isn't going to help make that happen, why would they print it?

The Internet is leveling the playing field for the little guy, but you still gotta be able to answer the questions that follow.

Who, What, When, Where and Wow!

●●

On day one of Journalism 101, you'd be told to focus on the *Who*, *What*, *When*, *Where*, *Why* and How of it all. But if you want to get to "Wow", you really have to start with Why.

WHY?

Why Do You Want Publicity?

*Y*ou gotta ask yourself, "What am I going for here?" More clients? More recognition? Increased hula hoop sales? Expert status? Or just the ego stroking that comes with seeing your name in lights? Not to mention the ancillary bragging rights that accrue to your mom.

This is critical 'cause, like everything else in life, if you know what you're going for, you're more likely to get it.

The next step is to ask yourself if publicity is the best way to get what you're going for.

> *The Pro is that you might get really well known. The Con is that you might get really well known!*

There Are Pros and Cons to Publicity

The *Pro* is that you might get really well known.
The *Con* is that you might get really well known!

Yeah, publicity is free, sort of, but have you really considered what getting well known might do to your life? You don't have to be Angelina Jolie to realize you're going to give up some privacy. You may not have people going through your garbage bins or shooting backyard photos from a helicopter with a zoom lens, but you may be recognized zipping out to pick up a bag of milk at the variety store in your torn sweatpants. There will be times when you might prefer to remain anonymous, like when you're screaming at your kid in the grocery store or having a drink with a friend at Hooters.

They Don't Call It "Exposure" For Nothing

People you've never met will know personal things about you. When my kids were little, one of the moms from school called to arrange a play date. When I told her my name she said "Are you that lawyer who left law to be a singer?" People will know stuff about you, your background, your dreams and aspirations, things you might feel perfectly comfortable having strangers read, but not necessarily your neighbors. I love it when people recognize me when I'm "out there", but I find it a little weird when I'm not in the mood to be known. Something to consider.

What Am I, Chopped Liver?

Not everybody minds the intrusion.

I read somewhere that upon leaving a movie premiere several years ago, a Hollywood starlet (not mentioning any names, but if you guessed that her name rhymes with Karen Kone, you'd be right) was disappointed to see that the paparazzi hadn't noticed her. So she went back to the theater and tried again. No luck. On her third and final trip, she got noticed, and harassed, as planned.

• • •

The main question with publicity is always *what*? What's your story? What's your angle? What makes you spotlight-worthy? But before we dive into the meat of it, let's get a few other important questions out of the way: *When*, *Who* and *Where*.

WHEN?

When Should You Seek Publicity?

*M*aybe you've heard it before — don't publicize till you're ready. Not only do you have to know what you're selling, but you also have to be ready to sell it. Sounds obvious, but many people jump into the spotlight too soon.

Let's say you score big time and get your local paper to do a feature article about you as a photographer. Next day, a reader calls and asks to see your portfolio. *"Uh, yes, well, I'm in the process of putting it together; no, my web site is still under construction. My studio? Yes, you could stop by, but we won't be finished renovations till next month...*

"Not very impressive. Wait till all the pieces (or at least most — it'll never be all) are in place so you can benefit from the exposure.

Timing is Everything!

So, let's say you're set up and ready to roll. The next question is "Is the world ready for you?" Many ideas die because they're ahead of their time; others are old news. As with most things in life, with publicity, timing is everything. What's fascinating today is often "been there, done that" by tomorrow. Or as my kids say "Mom, that's so last year!"

Bursting onto the Scene

What makes something newsworthy is that it's new, interesting, inspiring, unique, uncommon or original. Once the public has heard your story, they've heard it. Since you only get a few chances to burst onto the scene, everything has to be timed to work together. There has to be a specific goal for the publicity, and it's best to get all the wheels in motion simultaneously to reap the benefits.

Don't try to hog the stage! Once you've had a round of publicity, you gotta wait till there's a new story (or at least till you can create one). Till then, lay low. There are many that'll disagree with me on this one, but if you ask me, you can't burst onto the scene when you've been hanging around on the stage all along. The media doesn't need to be informed every time you've had a haircut. Be on for a while. Blow 'em away. Then lay low and allow the momentum to build again.

> The media doesn't need to be informed every time you've had a haircut.

Set Up the Dominoes

Because you want everything to fall into place at once, make sure all the dominoes are set up before you let the first one drop. Otherwise, you may get four dominoes into it and have to stop and take a few weeks to set up the fifth one and then the momentum is lost; the synergy is gone.

No point in an article coming out before you have distribution for your book or customers may give up trying to find it by the time it makes its way to the shelves. If you can time an article or interview to appear a week before the publication date or book launch, a few weeks before your national book tour, and around the time you have seven radio interviews, you'll have more impact. This part is tricky because with publicity, unlike advertising, the timing is not ultimately within your control.

One of my editors tells the story of an author who was a master of aligning the dominoes. The guy was a management consultant who worked in the high tech industry. After signing up a half dozen high profile clients to participate in his exclusive research study, he approached a publisher about writing a book on the results. With the commitment of the publisher, he then offered his clients the option of putting the book into the hands of all their senior managers at minimal cost, thus guaranteeing book sales upon publication.

The next domino was his arrangement to do a presentation at one of the industry's most important annual conferences, offering the conference attendees, 200-300 movers and shakers in the industry, the chance to be among the first to hear his findings, after his clients who were first in line.

The guy also made the conference organizers an offer they couldn't refuse, hosting a wine and cheese reception immediately following his late afternoon session, where he'd be on hand to autograph and sell his just-released book. A couple of hundred "guests" were invited to his book launch who were pumped by his speech and motivated to buy his book. Of course, media were also invited to both events — his conference address and the book launch.

The result? The guy not only sold a whole bunch of books, he helped solidify his reputation as one of the "thought-leaders" in his industry, eventually commanding $60,000 for keynote addresses around the world. And that's nothing to sneeze at!

Get Your Act Together

So, recap. Before you can even set up the dominoes, you gotta have your Publicity Department set up. You have to prepare all your promotional materials and have distribution of your product in place and any events confirmed. The more lead time you give yourself, the bigger the potential bang at the end. This is all about building momentum.

Timelines

It's crucial to research the timelines for every type of media you're targeting. Contact radio, TV, magazines and newspapers and find out how long it takes from the time a story idea is pitched till it ends up in print or on the air. This will vary widely even within a certain type of medium and also depends on the frequency of publication or broadcast.

Remember, you only get a few kicks at the can in any particular publication, often only one, and then, only if you're lucky, so you gotta prepare like crazy to get all the wheels in motion and do it all simultaneously to reap the benefits. (Think plate spinning on a unicycle.) If it's done too slowly or too quickly or the underpinnings aren't all in place, you won't hit the big time.

WHO?

Who Should be Your Publicist?
....

*N*ot always obvious...

Should You Hire a Pro?
....

Many people hire publicists to do their publicity for them. If you're busy and have the money, this can be a good option. Publicists are better connected to the media than you are and hopefully have earned their trust and developed a rapport. Publicists have a better chance of getting their phone calls returned and their press releases read. They're more experienced at preparing the necessary "paper" and they know the ropes.

Should You Be Your Own Publicist?
....

That said, there are a lot of reasons to be your *own* publicist.

One benefit of *not* "knowing the ropes" is that you'll probably break a few rules. Once you know the rules, it'll be a lot harder for you to break them and as we've already established, stars break the rules!

Also, a successful publicist will likely have many clients. You'll be competing with those other clients for the publicist's attention. Unless you can find a publicist who's just starting out and who'll devote his full day to promoting you, you may be better off doing it yourself. Rarely will anyone believe in your business more than you do.

Another limitation of professional publicists is that their success is determined by their credibility with the media. This means that a publicist who concentrates on the music industry can't put his reputation on the line every day for every client. He can't tell his contacts, "This is the best CD I've ever heard", every day, about every CD.

Some publicists will only take on clients they really believe in. If you're accepted as a client by one of these, you'll have a better chance of great results. But if a publicist only takes on one or two clients per category, he may have no better chance to develop contacts than you. Many publicists concentrate on one industry for precisely this reason.

How much better might it be if your publicist had only one client to promote? I once had a publicist tell me that I got more publicity for myself than she gets for her clients. The reason? She has the connections, but I have only one client, me.

No publicist can guarantee results. Despite best efforts, a publicist may not succeed in getting many, or even any, articles published or radio and TV interviews lined up. And you'll usually still have to pay for his efforts.

Then, there's the issue of cost. If you're a new business owner, you may have more time, drive, ambition and enthusiasm, than money. Although being your own publicist is a lot of work, if you educate yourself, you can potentially get the same or even better results than a publicist. And while it's true that, initially, you may not have the same access to the big publications as a professional would, this may be a good thing. Your message and image will evolve in the early years. You may be thankful, two or three years down the road, that your first TV appearance was on *Good Morning Chattanooga* rather than *Oprah* so that you have a chance to get comfortable on camera before appearing live in front of zillions of people.

The Third Option — Groom Your Own

There's a third option between hiring a publicist and doing it yourself. I know a singer who had a fan who was "between engagements". This fan, running on enthusiasm alone, became the singer's personal publicist and manager, with great success for both of them.

Why not groom your own publicist? You could find a local college or university student who's interested in working for you as an intern, usually for free or for a modest honorarium. Journalism students are ideal because they're looking for opportunities to make contact with the press and hone their writing skills. One of my former interns is now the entertainment editor at a city newspaper. The important thing to remember is that you're looking for a person with a different perspective than yours — and a way with words wouldn't hurt. The intern gets real life experience and you get over the initial hurdle of having to toot your own horn.

You Can Always Hire a Publicist Later

Once you've had 10-20 articles written in local and regional papers, you can then go to a publicist with materials in hand and get her to try to "take you national". By this time, you'll understand your market better, you'll be more experienced at giving interviews and you will have assembled a more impressive press kit, which'll give the publicist something to work with, cutting down on time (and therefore money) spent.

Who Should Be the Contact Person?
....

Even if you decide to open your own in-house publicity department, you gotta consider who is the best person to be your front man with the media; who'll make the calls to the media and be the contact name given on the press release? Many people enlist spouses, nannies or friends. Just make sure that the person you choose is great on the phone and can sell your story as well or better than you can.

If you're really stuck with "me, myself and I", you may consider making yourself look more like a star by putting a bit of distance between you and the media. I'll bet Stephen King doesn't spend his days calling local newspapers pitching articles about himself.

I know some performers (OK, OK, I confess!) who make the calls using a pseudonym, i.e., pretending to be their own publicist. This is a risky game and if it backfires it can blow up in your face. I started promoting my CD as Sue, because it's a lot easier to tell everyone what a great singer Tsufit is when you're playing someone else. I even made note of the pitch of my voice (high pitched for Sue, a little more mellow for Tsufit) on the index cards I kept for each contact. I usually got away with it because the segment producer who interviewed me on the phone was not the TV show host who interviewed me on the air, but I did have a few close calls.

This worked for me, and I know other people who've done it, (I have an amazing story for you later in this chapter — keep reading...), but you have to have nerves of steel. Be careful. Journalists aren't stupid. They're there to get the story and if the story is that you're messing with them, you're done!

Who Should Appear in the Spotlight?

Under normal circumstances, the answer to this question is "you". You're publicizing yourself as a person, artist, entrepreneur, business owner, etc. On the other hand, it may not be you that you want to promote. You may want to shine the spotlight solely on your business or perhaps on the star scientist at your firm. It may, in fact, be only your product which you're interested in publicizing, i.e., a revolutionary new soap bar which sunscreens you while showering. It can get hot under the lights. Make sure you're up for it. If not, find someone or something that is.

> *Director*
> 86-year-olds and 13-year-olds read different magazines and watch different TV shows. The only thing they might have in common is their bedtime.

Who's Your Ideal Audience?

What audience do you want to play to and why? The more you know about the audience you're trying to attract, the easier it'll be to attract them.

OK, so the accountants out there are asking, didn't she tell us, in Chapter 3, that we didn't have to worry if we don't know who our market is? Yeah, I said it, but you might want to hold off on seeking publicity till you've made some observations about who has chosen to seat themselves in your audience. Are they all 86 with grey hair or 13-year-olds with braces? 'Cause 86-year-olds and 13-year-olds read different magazines and watch different TV shows. The only thing they might have in common is their bedtime. It'll be easier to reach them if you know who they are. If you're still really in the dark, you may want to wait till you have a better idea or target general wide-audience publications, like daily newspapers, till you know more.

There's no point trying to get an article about your gold lamé thong bathing suit collection printed in a local Greek Orthodox newspaper or in an actuarial science journal. Sounds obvious, but people often send out press releases without a clue about the appropriateness of where they're sending them.

If you've been in business for a while you've probably made some observations. How old is your audience? Do they wear iPods or Depends? Are they male or female? Gay or straight? Do they go salsa dancing downtown on Saturday night or stay home with the kids and fold laundry? Do they watch *The Simpsons*, *Dateline NBC* or channel surf for the latest escapades of Paris Hilton?

> There's no point trying to get an article about your gold lamé thong bathing suit collection printed in a local Greek Orthodox newspaper or in an actuarial science journal.

There are lots of fascinating books out there to help you understand your market. Don't be afraid to go beyond the conventional marketing texts. Author Michael J. Weiss, the "Demographic Detective", has published a couple of groundbreaking books on the concept of "The Clustered World". Forget "Baby Boomers" and "Blue Collar Workers". He's come up with 62 different "clusters", including "Norma Rae-ville" and "Blue-Blood Estates", groups of people who may have more in common with their "cluster cousins" across the country than their immediate neighbors. Well worth checking out.

Got your "who"? Let's talk "where".

WHERE?

Where Do You Want to Publicize?

*T*he *who* and *where* questions tend to overlap when you're planning a publicity campaign, but let's get geographical for a minute.

Let's Get Geographical

Consider where you want to be known. Do you want to be known locally, regionally, in your state, nationally or internationally? Kinda depends what you're going for. A local pub might be happy to establish itself in a particular neighborhood, while a financial planner in Houston may benefit from a national profile, which brings with it increased credibility and the ability to charge bigger bucks. And, it's true that the world is a much smaller place than it was a few years ago.

Your choice of where to publicize depends, once again, on your goals in publicizing and where you're prepared to service or sell to. If you don't have distribution of your gadget in the U.K., there may be no point in seeking reviews there, unless you're hoping to attract a foreign distributor.

Starting Small
••••••••••••••••••••

Most media experts advise that you start publicity campaigns locally, where it's easier to get attention, and work your way up to regional, state wide, national and international, if they go that far. You can work your way outwards in concentric circles. If privacy is an issue for you, you may want to skip your hometown altogether. This isn't generally done because the hometown angle is usually the easiest card to play to get your first few interviews. The regional media may even be suspicious if nothing's been written about you in your own backyard. On the other hand, the hardest people to impress are usually the ones who already know you. With an Internet connection pretty much in every tent in the desert, you could choose to skip local and go international right away. Lots to consider.

Print, Radio, TV or Cyberspace?
••

The lines between the various types of media are continually getting blurrier and, ideally, you'll want to seek a combination of all types but you still gotta consider what kind of media works best for you.

Print is great 'cause you can blow up a newspaper article to poster size and feature it prominently in your restaurant.

TV is glamorous, but you often have to go to the station, sometimes a thousand miles away, possibly at 3 A.M. On the other hand, reruns are nice. I was in the shower in a Holiday Inn in Montreal with my kids in front of the TV when they yelled "Mommy come quick! You're on TV in Montreal!" The documentary about me keeps rerunning in different markets and I even get royalties for the songs I wrote that were featured.

Radio, you can do in your pajamas and you can even keep cheat sheets in front of you so you remember what you want to say on the air. It's less likely than TV to get edited, so it's easier to slip in a plug, but it's also less likely to get rebroadcast.

The Internet offers you the chance to launch your own show or magazine, if you can get over the whole "needle in a haystack" thing.

The "Blogosphere" has already had such an impact; it's changing the face of publicity as we know it. Truth be told, I was tempted to slash this whole chapter down to 5 words: "Go hang out with bloggers!"* If you're lucky, they'll talk about you so much that you'll be in a position to tell Oprah, "Sorry, O, next Tuesday isn't really good for me."

Lots to consider, but first you gotta figure out *what* you want to publicize. This is where the fun begins.

*Check out the Appendix for a list of some of the many fabulous marketing blogs out there.

WHAT?

What Should You Publicize?

F iguring out what to publicize is where we separate the stars from the "also rans".

Getting publicity, if you're not particular about what kind of publicity, is easy. You can get publicity by running around naked in public. Remember "streakers"? But is this the kind of publicity you want?

Bet Mel Gibson's having a few second thoughts about making headlines, in 2006, with "Mel's Big Meltdown".

> *Getting publicity, if you're not particular about what kind of publicity, is easy. Remember "streakers"?*

Don't Publicize the Wrong Message

You only get one chance to make a good first impression. OK, so I didn't make that one up. But it's true. Comedic actors have a hard time being taken seriously as actors because the public pigeonholes them as comics. Consider what image you're trying to project. If you change your message too often, the public gets confused. And as I said earlier, "You confuse, you lose". Once again, do your trial and error off Broadway. Once you're known to be a star in one arena, you can attempt to cross over.

What's Your Angle?

In my publicity seminars, we play a game show called "What's My Angle?"™ We have three contestants compete to come up with the best publicity angle for the guest (a randomly selected participant). Each contestant takes a turn asking the guest one question and the contestants continue till one of them shouts out an interesting headline for a newspaper article or TV interview. The audience (representing the media and ultimately the reading public) judges the headlines by applause, till one of the angles is declared the winner.

Try playing this game with your friends or colleagues till you get very creative about coming up with a good angle and headline. The first press release I sent to the media was captioned "Litigation Lawyer Leaves Law for Limelight". My second campaign was about "Bringing Color to Business" and was punctuated by the colorful clothes I wore and the colorful language I used in the release. The campaign resulted in headlines like "Tsufit — Teaching the World to Dream in Technicolor" and "True Colors".

Hook, Line and Headline

In order to grab 'em, you need a hook. What's a hook? It's the thing that pulls the reader to read and the viewer to view. We're used to hearing hooks every day. It's what the

TV show host says, just before cutting to commercial, about what's going to be on the show after the break: "'10 Ways to Find Out if Your Husband's Cheating on You', after the break…" or "'Why Watching Lots of TV Will Make Your Kid a Whiz in Biz', on tomorrow's show".

In print media, the hook is usually the headline. On the Internet, it's the little teaser on a site's home page that entices you to click through for more information.

There are basically two categories of media coverage, news and human interest, but there are many more specific kinds of hooks. Here's a list of 25 hooks to get you started. It's not comprehensive and many categories overlap, but it's a great exercise to see how many of these hooks you can come up with for your business. Invite some friends over, order pizza, and play "Hookmania"™, my brainstorming game. (It's the "What's My Angle?"™ home edition.)

Here are the hooks.

1. The News Hook
2. The Controversy Hook
3. The Observation Hook
4. The Event Hook
5. The Trend Hook
6. The Seasonal Hook
7. The "Always in Season" or "Evergreen" Hook
8. The "None of Our Business, But We Want to Know Anyway" Hook
9. The Celebrity Hook
10. The "Celebrity Once Removed" Hook
11. The "Look Who's Wearing My Stuff!" Hook
12. The "Inspirational/Overcoming Adversity" Hook
13. The "Saving the Kid at the Bottom of the Well" Hook
14. The "Cute and Corny, I'll Help You Fill Your Extra Newspaper Space" Hook

15. The "Too Crazy to Be True" Hook
16. The Contest Hook
17. The Survey Hook
18. The "First, Last, Youngest, Oldest, Newest, Biggest, Smallest, Skinniest, Fattest, Shortest, Tallest..." Hook
19. The "Show and Tell" Hook
20. The Charity Hook
21. The "Crook" Hook
22. The Best Hook of All (But, I Won't Tell You Yet...)
23. The "Underdog" or "Ordinary Guy" Hook
24. The "Make Up Your Own Holiday" Hook
25. The "Something Out of Nothing" Hook

Yes, Virginia, the type of hook you select does make a difference, and hook selection depends on the species of fish being sought.

saltfishing.about.com

1. The News Hook
••••••••••••••••••••••

You can catch three species with this particular hook.

- **The "About to Happen, Anticipatory" News Hook.** Sounds dopey almost a decade later, but back in December 1999, the world was more worried than Cinderella about what would happen when the clock struck midnight. There were opportunities galore for bankers, computer consultants and authors, both before January 1, 2000, (making predictions) and after (commenting on what happened or, more accurately, what didn't).
- **The "Something Big Just Happened" Hook.** After a tragic event, psychiatrists are always in demand to explain why the "nice guy next door"

did the horrific thing he did or to counsel the victims. The best time to watch the news is at 3 A.M. That's when the media is furiously working on the morning show and you can catch them at their desks with a last minute tie-in on a breaking story or save the day by offering yourself as an expert source.

- **The "Tie-In With an Old Story" Hook.** "Just Unveiled: New Evidence Shows Man Evolved From Giraffes, Not Apes. Zookeeper joins us, after the break." This one also fits into the next category.

2. The Controversy Hook

"The Oldest Child: Leader or Bully?" or "Are Short Children Really Dumber?" or "Are Carrots Killing Us? Nutritionist Tells Us Why Carrots Are Worse Than Candy." We're not talking Jerry Springer here, but being provocative gets ratings.

Elvis did rather nicely with this one when Ed Sullivan refused to film him from the waist down. Or when radio D.J.s were filmed smashing his records because they were "the devil's music".

3. The Observational Hook

"Why Are Most CEO's Six Feet Tall? Does Your Short Kid Stand a Chance?" A psychologist or HR professional could cash in on this one, as could a short CEO.

Here are a couple of real ones I saw recently on the Internet.

"Astounding News About Left-Handed Men". It seems that left-handed college graduates earn 26% more than the rest of us. Not true for women lefties.

"A Very Strange Fact About Blue-Eyed Men". Apparently blue-eyed men prefer blue-eyed women to those with chocolate eyes like me. According to Netscape, researchers in Norway think it has to do with genetics. Since a blue-on-blue union should produce a baby-blue, if the baby has brown eyes, it might raise the suspicion that maybe the postman does too... I have a client who's in the eye business, an iridologist. She could have a field day with this stuff!

4. The Event Hook
••••••••••••••••••••••

It's always great to have an event to publicize. The mandate of most media is to cover what's going on. An event adds immediacy to your story. If you don't have an event, consider whether you should create one so that your story will have a time anchor. Otherwise, even if you can get a publication interested in the fact that you have 38 dogs living with you, there's no urgency for the magazine to print your story.

On the other hand, keep in mind that if your story is time anchored, you run the risk of being old news and missing the opportunity for any promotion. I was scheduled to appear in a national TV interview but I got bumped from Friday to the following Tuesday because Dr. Phil was unexpectedly available for my slot. If my story had been intended to tie-in with a concert that weekend, rather than the general feature it was, I might have lost the interview altogether. Your challenge is to gauge which approach gives you the greater chance of success.

Name Your Events: The Broccoli Tour

Musicians often name their tours. When I planned a series of concerts around the province, I named the concert "Broccoli's on Sale at Dominion", after one of the comedic songs (maybe you've heard of it...) in the show. The press release announced that, in the spirit of Madonna's Blonde Ambition Tour, I was going out on The Broccoli Tour. The releases went out on green paper with a little piece of broccoli clip art. Tacky as that sounds, vegetables get attention. One of the newspapers ran a feature article under the headline "Entertainer Launches Broccoli Tour" lifting the first paragraph straight from the press release, almost verbatim. It's unbelievable what kinda crazy stuff they'll print if you give 'em a good name.

Speaking of naming stuff, "Bennifer" was an intriguing way of referring to the short lived coupling of Ben Affleck and Jennifer Lopez. Affleck later married a different Jennifer (Garner) saddling that union with "Bennifer II". Check out "TomKat" for Tom Cruise and Katie Holmes. "Brangelina" for Pitt and Jolie. Naming a phenomenon that doesn't usually have a name ("Camelot" describing the Kennedy mystique) increases the cachet and the amount of press it gets. Going from Jennifer Lopez to "JLo" didn't hurt old "Jenny from the Block".

5. The Trend Hook

Be *trendy*. Stuff happens. Every day. Postal workers talk about going on strike, people get sick because of contaminated drinking water, postal workers go on strike, a city makes an Olympic bid, postal workers go on strike, car accidents get blamed on cell phones. People have concerns about loss of privacy, second hand smoke, purple-haired kids hanging around malls and red light cameras... There are thousands of these issues, issues like "cocooning" back in the 90s and low carb diets a few years ago, issues that are being discussed in the newspapers, in the parking lots and in our streets.

This could also be called the "Hot Issue" hook. You gotta make yourself irresistible to an editor. Take your message, your story, and creatively link it to something people are already talking about. But make sure it's current. Yesterday's "hot" is today's "lukewarm".

"Super Fries Me!"

You don't have to be a brain surgeon to figure out how to tie into a trend. The release of *Super Size Me*, a documentary about the dangers of living on fast food, was perfectly timed to be released during an era of regularly reported statistics concerning the epidemic of childhood obesity. *Super Size Me*, which was nominated for an Academy Award, may not have received much attention way back in the day when we were all more interested in what size shoes and gloves O.J. was wearing.

Super Size Me became one of the most successful documentaries of all time, not only because it rode the trend, but because of the controversy hook. Let's just say McDonald's wasn't pleased, which made viewers want to check it out for themselves. Throw in some stats and we're cookin'.

Would You Like Fries With That?

Why are Americans so fat? Find out in Super Size Me, a tongue in-cheek — and burger in hand — look at the legal, financial and physical costs of America's hunger for fast food.

Ominously, 37% of American children and adolescents are carrying too much fat and 2 out of every three adults are overweight or obese. Is it our fault for lacking self-control or are the fast-food corporations to blame?
www.rottentomatoes.com

Be On Alert

Even if you're a "mouse potato" and never leave your desk, you can keep current by subscribing to Google News Alerts. Type in a few key words in your subject area, an area you'd be prepared to comment on to the media, and every day, you can receive alerts about what's going on in the world, either a news item or a trend, which you could tie into.

Spice It Up With Stats

Do your research and find some statistics to support whatever you're saying. Or create surveys and come up with your own statistics. Next time you read a magazine or newspaper or listen to a segment on the radio or on TV, take note of how often they open with a statistic. Stats add weight to whatever you're commenting on.

6. The Seasonal Hook

The inventor of a solar-powered air conditioner should be getting his publicity materials together in the winter and seeking coverage during the first heat wave. A song I wrote, "My Transylvanian", gets lots of radio airplay every Halloween, just as the one I wrote about my mom gets played every Mother's Day. (Fourth mention if you're counting.) Up here in igloo country, every winter, it snows. Kinda predictable. I was just leafing through the winter edition of the national auto association magazine. (Clearly, I have too much time on my hands.) There was the predictable sidebar from the Physiotherapy Association reminding us how to properly shovel snow to avoid back injury. But there was also a more inventive winter tie-in, a piece headlined "Urban Cool", which described the "hottest thing" to hit the club scene, an Ice Lounge. It's a club built entirely out of ice, where patrons get parkas and gloves at the door. Note, that this wouldn't have received any ink in May or September, but makes a compelling story in January or July.

7. The "Always in Season" or "Evergreen" Hook
••••••••••••••••••••••

Other stories are always in season, like "10 Ways to Lose Weight in Your Sleep" or "How to Make Chocolate Chip Cookies Mrs. Fields Would Envy" or "How to Take Care of Our Bodies, Like We Take Care of Our Cars" or "The 5 Things Men Do That Drive Women Wild."

8. The "None of Our Business, But We Want to Know Anyway" Hook
••••••••••••••••••••••••••••

"What Did Brad Tell Angelina About Jennifer? What Did Trump Secretly Confess About Rosie When The Camera Wasn't Rolling? Limo Driver Gives Us Fly-on-the-Wall Look at the Inside Lives of the Rich and Famous". Good way for Joe's Limos to get noticed.

9. The Celebrity Hook

"Ashton: Demi and I Never Argue." Unbelievable, but that was an actual headline on my news home page. It goes on to explain, that they did have an argument once, but not till after the first three months. That's news? That's a story? Doesn't take much if you're a celeb.

How 'bout this one? "Find Out Which Celebrity Kids Bring In the Big Bucks". Apparently a photo of Gwyneth Paltrow and daughter Apple (wonder how "Apple" would score in the name popularity experiments) can get you over 100 grand!

10. The "Celebrity Once Removed" Hook

"Demi's Nanny Takes Kids for Ice-Cream. Story at 11." OK, I made that one up, but if you think I'm kidding about the "Celebrity Once Removed" Hook, do I have a story for you, in Chapter 6!

Certain entrepreneurs have made names for themselves by associating themselves with celebrities and as a result many have become celebrities themselves. There are celebrity hairdressers in Hollywood who are more famous than some of their clients.

Rubbing shoulders with celebrities rarely hurts a business, if you can pull it off. Roots' Michael Budman is a pro at this. What a coup to have famous young television stars and musicians wearing your leather jackets or Olympic athletes wearing your hats.

> If you're standing close enough to a celebrity, the spotlight may shine on you too.

Dr. Phil's life was never the same after Oprah retained the psychiatrist to coach her for her "tainted beef" courtroom drama. Now he's a celebrity himself.

Where there are celebrities, there are spotlights. If you're standing close enough to a celebrity, the spotlight may shine on you too.

Over a hundred million copies later, Jack Canfield tells the story of how he and Mark Victor Hansen sent *Chicken Soup for the Soul* books to jurors in the O.J. trial. That made the duo "celebrities twice removed". They figured the jurors were bored and couldn't read the newspaper. The jurors were also being photographed walking in and out of the courtroom. And guess what they were carrying under their arms?

You may not be looking to become a celebrity, but there's no doubt that the endorsement or even implied endorsement or reflected spotlight of a celebrity means money in the bank and clients in the waiting room.

11. The "Look Who's Wearing My Stuff!" Hook

They don't give an Oscar for it, but the "best dress" competition is every bit as fierce as the race for the Oscars themselves. *Advertising Age* reported that "In 2006, when advertisers paid $1.7 million for 30 seconds of airtime during the *Academy Awards* broadcast, designers were shelling out similar sums in the hope that one dress would end up on the red carpet." Why? 'Cause a 10-second celebrity interview, if the celebrity is wearing your dress or hat or purse or shoes can take you from oblivion to stardom yourself. And it's the gift that keeps on giving, 'cause the photos (with accompanying credits) will appear in doctors' waiting rooms for the next 99 years. Who can you send your stuff to? You don't have to dress the celeb.

How 'bout her dog? If Fifi gets 'caught on camera wearing your poodle coat, break out the champagne. Then you can label all your stuff with the label "As seen on ..."

How can you contact Sarah Jessica Parker to send her your topaz toe ring? Check out *www.contactany celebrity.com* for the most comprehensive listings on the planet.

12. The "Inspirational/Overcoming Adversity" Hook
....

"He overcame his fear of water to jump in and save five newborn kittens. Our next guest discusses how you can overcome lifelong fears in a split second."

If you climbed Mount Everest on a dare, barefoot and blindfolded with 10 monkeys on your head and it changed your life, you may have the makings of an inspirational human interest story.

13. The "Saving the Kid at the Bottom of the Well" Hook
....

Kinda self-explanatory. Most programmes throw one of these in whenever they can (no pun intended).

14. The "Cute and Corny, I'll Help You Fill Your Extra Newspaper Space" Hook
....

OK, so maybe this shouldn't be an official hook category, but you'd be surprised how many of these get printed when there's nothing else going on. (I've seen podiatrists score big on slow news days.) You recognize them, things like: "There's No Accounting for Taste" about an accountant who sells pickle-flavored ice cream on weekends.

15. The "Too Crazy To Be True" Hook

Why make 'em up when I can take them straight from the headlines? Hot news flash from Bejing: "Woman Crashes While Teaching Dog to Drive". Ripley made a career out of this stuff!

16. The Contest Hook

Once Buckley's mixture figured out that its claim to fame was its awful taste, it mounted a "Send Us Your Buckley's Face" campaign encouraging customers to send in a photo of themselves wincing from the bad taste. Visitors to their web site vote on the best faces. Winners get T-shirts. Something interesting created from nothing.

17. The Survey Hook

First cousin to the Contest Hook. You get one article where you ask 'em something and a second article where you tell 'em what they said. Not too shabby!

18. The "First, Last, Youngest, Oldest, Newest, Biggest, Smallest, Skinniest, Fattest, Shortest, Tallest..." Hook

Never overlook an easy angle. I have a client who is both a grandmother and a granddaughter at the same time, the crowning jewel in the middle of five generations of strong women. Throw in a photo of the 93-year-old great great grandmother teaching the seven-year-old great great granddaughter to make pasta sauce, with the three other mothers/daughters looking on, and you've got the makings of a great Mother's Day feature. This could run as a "Family That Cooks Together, Stays Together" article to contrast growing concerns about kids and drugs.

I have a client who has 8 kids. I thought that was a lot till I worked with another client who has 11 kids! 13 people in the family. Too bad she missed a tie-in with the release of Steve Martin's *Cheaper By The Dozen* movies. "How Entrepreneur Juggles Career and Home and Still Whips Up Homemade Burritos for 13!"

19. The "Show and Tell" Hook

This isn't really a hook by itself, but you may be able to "Show and Tell" your way onto the little screen. A magazine may just print a quick "How To" list as a sidebar or spin it into a larger article, but if you want to see your face on TV, you'll increase your chances if you can give the audience a demonstration. Nobody likes talking heads. Show us how to whip up an egg-free soufflé or make corn cob toilet seat covers and you may just get your 15 minutes of fame. Worked for Martha.

20. The Charity Hook

In addition to the many other obviously good reasons to hold events for charity, charitable events get media coverage. It's the media's way of contributing to the charity. So consider a charity tie-in.

I recognized this principle when I was a mere lass of 17. I had dreams of putting on a concert with another girl I was singing with at the time. I realized that if we made it a benefit concert, in addition to doing some good in the world, we'd be more likely to get publicity and free advertising, which we did. We even got the local camera store to sell tickets to the public. We corralled a band and friends to make posters, tickets and T-shirts with our names printed on them, but my dream was a big feature article in the newspaper.

I didn't know anything about press releases at that time, nor did we have any photos, but I did have the *chutzpah* to call the newspaper and tell them about our show being held at our high school. I don't know whether it was because we were donating all proceeds to the Cancer Society, or whether our youthful exuberance won over the editor, or merely the fact that no other 17-year-old had thought of calling the newspaper, but they sent out a photographer to our school and printed that photo together with an article headlined "Singing Schoolgirls — Graduation May End Their Act". The Beatles couldn't have asked for better!

Bob Geldof copied me. He did the same thing on a slightly larger scale. He pulled off the ultimate charity tie-in. Sir Geldof (don't know if he got the local camera store to sell tickets, but he did get knighted for his efforts) managed to mount two live televised concerts featuring 60 of the world's biggest rock stars to raise money for famine relief in Africa. A billion-and-a-half people around the world watched the 16 hour event on TV as over £100 million was raised. It made musical and political history.

As a member of the Boomtown Rats (now *there's* a name), Geldof was already a successful and moderately well known recording artist, but the Irish singer would surely never have made the cover of *Time* Magazine, been appointed to an Aids Panel with Bill Gates and UN Secretary General Kofi Annan or become a household name, if he hadn't stepped into the spotlight with the charity hook. While I'm sure the guy had purely altruistic motives, I doubt the publicity hurt him any.

Corporations recognize that charity is good business, not only because it keeps their name in the media, but because it builds their reputation as "good corporate citizens". M & M's candy teamed up with The Susan G. Komen Breast Foundation to produce special pink and white M & M's to raise money for the foundation. It got noted in the media and the charity link certainly won't hurt the M's.

21. The "Crook" Hook

We have an insatiable appetite for stories about criminals and the crimes they commit, especially the dumb ones. Tie your story to criminal activity and you'll get a piece of the action, attention-wise. Better if you're not personally involved in the aforementioned criminal activity... I just saw an expert being interviewed on TV, after the recovery of a kidnap victim, to explain why victims get attached to their captors. No one wants to feel like an ambulance chaser, but there is a publicity opportunity around every corner.

22. The Suspense Hook

So, were you dying to know which hook this was going to be? That's the whole point, the "Dying to Know" part. "Will They or Won't They?" "You Won't Believe Who The Donald Fired Now!" Notice how the headlines in the Observation Hook are phrased to make us click on that link. It's the same principle we used in writing the info-mercials. Suspense works. The mind can't stand an incomplete puzzle. Inquiring minds want to know. Give us only half the story and we're...hooked!

23. The "Underdog" or "Ordinary Guy" Hook

Check out a documentary called *My Date With Drew*. Synopsis: Ordinary guy, out of shape, broke, has had crush on actress Drew Barrymore since her *ET* days. Out of work, he sets a goal of getting Drew to go out on a date with him. He enlists his friends to help him document his quest with a video camera "on loan" from a store until the 30-day return period ends. Long story short. Viral Internet marketing campaign kicks in and he gets his dream date with Drew and tons of publicity — I'm talkin' *Chicago Sun Times, Entertainment Tonight, Hollywood Reporter, Variety* and tons more. Why all the fuss? 'Cause he's the underdog. And more importantly, 'cause he's one of us. We all see ourselves in Ordinary Guy. And if he can do it, we can too. Powerful hook!

24. The "Make Up Your Own Holiday" Hook

The greeting card companies have been doing this for years. It's time regular folk got a piece of the action. One author did. She created a special day for stay at home moms (about bloody time) called "Please Take My Children to Work Day". She got 6 U.S. governors to proclaim the holiday (only in America) and she's become a media darling — *The New York Times, USA Today, The Los Angeles Times, Parenting, The Washington Post* — this stuff really works.

What if you've got nothing? How do you take a blatant commercial message, which is really just ad material, and make news with it? Let me give you one last hook. (There are millions more where this came from. Once you start, it's hard to stop.)

25. The "Make Something Out of Nothing" Hook

The neat thing about this one is that it gets you around the rule that there has to be a story. What you do is you *create* the story, by creating an "event" or more accurately, a publicity stunt. This is Hook #4 on steroids.

Publicity Stunts

We've all heard of publicity stunts, public stunts performed for the sole purpose of generating publicity. Janet Jackson's wardrobe malfunction comes to mind. Not sure about Janet, but if the stunt is creative, intrigues your audience or simply lets them know you exist without harming your credibility, go for it!

Taking the Plunge

WonderBra sent 100 beautiful half naked women into the streets of London, England, in just a black bra and panties to promote the new WonderBra Multi-Plunge Bra. If this company, as well known as it is, had just sent out a press release about this product, it probably would have been tossed into the garbage. It's not news, but 100 women, in their underwear, posing in the middle of the street in front of the National Gallery to demonstrate the 100 ways to wear the new bra? The women literally stopped traffic, and the result was that I ended up reading about it all the way over in North America. Talk about accessing your inner *chutzpah!*

And that, folks, is how it's done. Something out of nothing. You want another example?

Kiss and Tell
....

Hershey's managed to make headlines "to celebrate the pairing of smooth milk chocolate and creamy, luscious caramel" in their new Hershey's kisses. And to think we might have missed that earth shattering event! Yet Hershey's managed to grab some ink, not to mention cyber-ink. They partnered with movie theaters and *Us Weekly* to choose "The Top 10 Best Kisses on Film". (Molly Ringwald made the list twice, right up there with Clark Gable, Omar Sharif, and Humphrey Bogart. Molly Ringwald???)

They sweetened the event with "Did They or Didn't They?" *Apprentice* finalists, Amy Henry (who not coincidently had a book to promote) and Nick Warnock sharing a public smooch in front of a huge Hershey's Kiss on top of the Empire State Building. (This is a creative cocktail of the "Create an Event" Hook, the "Celebrity" Hook, the "Contest" Hook, the "Something Out of Nothing" Hook and the "None of Our Business" Hook all rolled into one.)

• • •

Send a Suitcase of M & M's
....

Publicity seekers build pitches (like infomercials) around these hooks and are often very innovative about how they deliver them. Get creative and access your inner *chutzpah*. When in doubt, send a suitcase of M & M's.

You think I'm kidding? Word on the street is that a Canadian comedian was trying to get the attention of a TV producer, but he was afraid of being lost in all the phone calls and paper that producers get daily, so the guy spent 75 big ones on a faux leather briefcase and filled it with 50 pounds of M & M's. He wrapped the briefcase with the words, "Bribe Enclosed" and couriered it to the producer. The comedian got a call the next day and ended up on the show. Never underestimate the power of well targeted chocolate.

If You Can't Take the Heat, Get Out of the Kitchen
••••••••••••••••••••••••••••••

You have to really loosen up to come up with this stuff, hard for people who spend their days preparing financial statements or legal briefs, as I used to do. Recently, one of my clients, who's an executive chef, consulted me to inspire her to write some promo material. She's cooked for Will Smith and trained with Martha Stewart, so we threw that in for starters. A little celebrity name dropping never hurts, but that wasn't enough. Her mission is to teach the world about "live cuisine", i.e., preparation of sumptuous meals without any cooking. Since no heating of food is involved, we drummed up the "Throw Out Your Stove" campaign.

She'll write the *Throw Out Your Stove Cookbook*, teach Throw Out Your Stove Cooking Classes and give consultations to health spas and upscale restaurants about creating a Throw Out Your Stove Menu. We talked about creating printed materials featuring a "de-stoved" kitchen with an easy chair or a palm tree in the little square space where the stove usually goes together with Throw Out Your Stove bumper stickers and pins — like those "No Smoking" signs.

Her press release will describe this as a "movement", a natural progression from the bra burning women's liberation movement of the 60s. "You've come a long way, baby" indeed. She can throw in stats about the health benefits of eating "live foods", in a fashion similar to the

"Super Size Me" blurb, above. If she's really feeling feisty, she can try Hook 24 and declare "Throw Out Your Stove" Day, enlist some health organizations and magazines to back her up and have people send in photos of their stoves out on the curb. It's all kinda silly, and the result of a very brief brainstorming session, but her message (that we all should be eating more unprocessed uncooked foods to be healthy) will be heard.

Thinking Outside The Fridge

In Chapter 3, we discussed how you sell an ugly brown liquid. How 'bout a beautiful white one? Want a great example of 95 zillion ways to spin a story? Dairy farmers can do it till the cows come home! Check out the hugely successful "Got Milk?" campaign out of California (excerpts are from the Got Milk? web site). These dairy folk have got an angle on everything and it all leads to one conclusion. You gotta drink the white stuff!

Milking It!

- **Lovers?** Chai Latte, the "Valentine's Day drink of choice", contains spices which, in India, are "widely believed to be aphrodisiacs". "Love-in-a-cup".
- **Teens?** Girls skip breakfast "at a critical time in their lives, when most bone mass is accumulated". The solution? Drink milk.
- **Kids?** Apparently "half of California children ages 6 to 8 have untreated cavities". Not to worry. The dairy farmers have got your back. Just drink the cow juice. No surprises there.
- **Sports Types?** You don't have to shell out big bucks for fancy sports drinks. "Research reveals that

chocolate milk beats out other sports drinks hands down in helping athletes recover from intense workouts."

- **Sleep Deprived Americans?** Forget pills. "A protein in milk tells the brain to sleep."

They've even got an extraterrestrial angle! These guys aren't afraid to think outside the fridge!

● ● ●

It's said that the print media focuses on stories, whereas broadcast media (radio and TV) are all about the segment or the show. But one thing successful self-publicists agree on is that one of the best ways to get a leg-up is to help the producers and editors put the stuff together.

Pitch the Show, the Whole Show and Nothing But the Show!

Your job as your own publicist is to become a resource to the media, to get them to know, like and trust you, so that you'll get called when they're working on a story. One way to convey that message is by helping them put the show together.

Find Some Co-Stars

An inventor looking for a few minutes of fame should find a few other inventors and pitch a show on crazy inventions. He'll be much more likely to get his moment of glory than if he suggests a story about him alone. He could even suggest bringing on a famous inventor who's scored big on a crazy idea as a judge for the audience's invention ideas. (A similar concept did air as a series on television.)

Our limo driver could offer to bring makeup artists, bartenders and hairdressers with him for a segment called "What Celebs Say, When They Forget We're Here."

• • •

Got your hook? Good.

Now pull out any publicity "how to" book and knock out your media release and press kit. (See *www.your publicitydepartment.com* to get you started.)

Wanna see a dynamite example right away? Check out the 1-800-Got-Junk? site. Any show host could throw the CEO on the air tomorrow armed with the juicy stuff in that kit. They even have a list of the weird garbage they've removed from houses. Get this: 5 moose heads, 18,000 cans of expired sardines and a couch full of bees. Trust me, sardines *always* make for a good show.

So start working on your press kit. But first, I want to tell you something...

THE REAL SECRET — SSSHHH!

OK, here's the real secret of getting more publicity than you know what to do with. I've hidden it all the way in the back of this chapter, because only people who made it this far are likely to benefit from it.

The best kept secret to getting lots of great publicity is — *asking for it*!

Ask For It
••••••••••••••

Nine out of every ten entrepreneurs won't. They'll wish for it. They'll complain about not getting it, but they won't take the risk of *asking* for it.

When I was performing regularly at folk music festivals, I'd come into the city where the festival was taking place and there'd be a big feature article in the newspaper about the headline performer and a big feature article about me. The other 49 performers on the bill would wonder, "Why her? She's not famous".

They knew that and *I* knew that, but the people in town who read the paper didn't know that. All the readers knew was that my face was plastered all over the paper along with the headliner. This scenario played itself out, over and over and over again, in almost every city I went into.

The big secret of my success? *I asked.*

Headliners have publicists working for them. I have me. I contact the editor of the paper and the local news radio and TV stations in the city I'm going to perform in a couple of months before the festival and introduce myself. I pitch them my story, telling them that I'll be coming to perform in their city in a couple of months. A little bit of charm, a little story, a little *chutzpah,* and voilà, full color photos above the fold!

One Last Secret

I know, I only promised you one. But this is the one that'll get you the beach house. It's not a secret in show-biz, but for some reason, most entrepreneurs didn't get the memo.

Build Your Own Fan Club

One of the best ways to attract the media is to attract fans. If you have fans, the media will come, often on its own initiative, just to see what all the fuss is about. So, before you even contact the media, start building your own fan club.

Even if you aren't planning to pursue media for a while, you need your fan list to promote your core business. Showbiz needs "bums in seats". The hotel industry needs "heads in beds". Whatever you call 'em in your business, you need to collect the names of people who are interested enough in what you do to show up when you do it.

Your fan club isn't gonna build itself. You gotta build it — one name at a time. From the second you decide to go into business for yourself, begin collecting the names, addresses, telephone numbers and e-mail addresses of anyone who expresses interest in what you do.

Many years ago, I sang at a popular folk club. I thought my job was to show up and be amazing. How naïve I was. After one modestly attended performance, the owner called me aside and told me to "B.Y.O.F." (Bring Your Own Fans). And now I do.

Your Fans. Don't Leave Home Without 'Em

I was walking down 7th Avenue in New York City recently and I came across an endless line of "I wanna be a rapper" teenage boys camped out on the street a few blocks away from Madison Square Gardens. I was wondering if they were lined up for concert tickets or an *American Idol* audition, so I stopped and asked. Nope. They were lined up for something much more exciting — the midnight release of a new running shoe!

Think back to the last time you went into a music store. Did you go in as a customer or a fan?

Customer implies that a person walks into a store wanting to buy a CD and decides, after scanning the thousands

> *Director*
> After one modestly attended performance, the owner called me aside and told me to "B.Y.O.F." (Bring Your Own Fans). And now I do.

of albums available, which one to snatch up. A fan
walks into the store with the intent of buying the latest
Alanis Morissette CD....

Roger Blackwell and Tina Stephan,
Brands That Rock

So here's the question. Which CD would you rather
be, one of the thousands, sitting on the rack, impotently
screaming "pick me, pick me", or the CD that a fan went
into the store already planning to buy?

That's the difference a fan club can make, the difference
between browsers who might, if you're lucky, turn into
customers versus "fist-full-of-cash" pre-sold buyers, "sleep-
on-the-street" fans, looking for *you* and only you.

Marketing From The Market

Musician, Loreena McKennitt, understands the power of
a mailing list. While busking outside St. Lawrence Market
in Toronto, she collected names of passers-by who were
interested in her music. Having no budget for formal
publicity, she worked her list, keeping her fans up to date
about what she was up to. By the time she released her
self-produced album, she had created such a following
that she sold 100,000 albums on her own. Now, 13 million
albums later, this double platinum recording artist is still
self-produced and runs her own label.

I promised you an amazing story. Here it is.

Hitting the Top of the Charts!

Performers have always understood the power of having a
following, but the real power always rested with traditional
media, newspapers, radio and television, because of their

broad reach. Nowadays, 22-year-olds with lap tops are bringing traditional media to its knees.

I met a very interesting guy recently, a well dressed man in a business suit who calls himself an "Internet marketer". Former vacuum cleaner salesman turned multi-millionaire, Armand Morin decided to apply his Internet marketing savvy to the cause of an unknown country music artist named Michael Lee Austin. Morin believes in speed and his credos are "Success Leaves Traces" and "Create Your Own Reality", but it's not just motivational mumbo jumbo. That's exactly what he does. He creates his own reality.

With record companies spending millions of dollars to launch their artists' CDs, Morin's artist, Michael Lee Austin, debuted at #7 on *Billboard's* Internet Music Chart and #63 on *Billboard's* Overall Country Music Chart. Incredible for a first-time, unknown artist! Austin hit #1, in just a few hours, at *Amazon.com*, and had the best-selling CD at Amazon for four solid days, beating out heavyweights like Bruce Springsteen and Tim McGraw.

How did he do it? He built a huge e-mail list worldwide. One name at a time. He used "Squeeze Pages" and e-zines and Press Releases and partnered with other marketers who had lists. Then, one day, they all clicked "Send" on their computers simultaneously and the rest is history.

Wait. The story gets better! Armand was using the "Sue sells Tsufit" technique I told you about earlier. *Billboard*–charting, country-music singer, Michael Lee Austin, is none other than — drum roll, please — suit and cufflinks guy, businessman, Armand Morin, in a cowboy hat! (For a bit of fun, check out the web sites and compare photos.)

Huge multi-national corporations are starting to take notice of Internet marketing techniques. Find some of these guys who know how to build a solid opt-in mailing list and pay them whatever they ask to teach you.

Build a blog. Better yet, get to know other bloggers. *New York Times* bestselling author, Tim Ferriss, credits online marketing, and in particular blogs, with catapulting his book, *The 4-Hour Workweek*, onto bestseller lists, before conventional publicity had even kicked in. His book hit the *New York Times* Bestseller List in just 4 days after its release. Not too shabby!

Authors and speakers are always being told to build themselves a platform. Good advice. Ask any rock star. He who has his own fans will never go hungry. Build yourself a fan base. And name them. The "Soul Patrol" helped Taylor Hicks win *American Idol*. Clay Aiken doesn't go anywhere without his "Claymates". Build yourself a flock. A following. A herd.

> Build yourself a flock. A following. A herd. The power is in the list.

The secret? "The power is in the list."

OK, so maybe you're thinking, "Yeah, rock stars and motorcycles are sexy. How am I gonna get fans for my accounting practice?"

Anyone can do this. Check this out.

You are cordially invited to attend our annual reunion to be held in the Royal York Hotel in downtown Toronto. The gala event will include dinner, entertainment, camaraderie, and an examination of your hernia repair.

Quoted by Ben McConnell and Jackie Huba in
Creating Customer Evangelists

Yes folks, even a hernia hospital can do this!

(I don't make this stuff up!) A Canadian hospital, let's just call them "House of Hernia", they've been doing this since 1948! They've had over a quarter of a million patients and they get 'em together, 1000 of them, for a bit of dinner, dancing and fun. (I hear they leave them in stitches...)

They've got fans! And one report documented that 49% of their new patients, almost half, are referrals from former patients. Fans bringing new fans!

There are multi-million selling authors and musicians who don't know who their fans are. That means they have to work much harder to stay visible so their fans can find them. Keep a list and keep in touch.

When to Turn Down Publicity

There is a saying in showbiz: "There is no such thing as bad publicity". The theory is that people talking about you is always a good thing. And often it is.

The Bare Naked Ladies, who were neither naked nor ladies, caused quite a stir when the good citizens of Toronto protested against a band with a name like that playing in their public square in front of City Hall. This controversy helped put the "Ladies" on the national radar. Not too shabby for a group that only a few years earlier could be seen up close and personal in the local bars.

And Madonna seems to thrive on controversy. In 1990, the Toronto police threatened to arrest Madonna if she didn't change the "Like a Virgin" segment of her Blonde Ambition Tour. She didn't change it, didn't get arrested and the media coverage only added to her mystique.

However, for most of us, there is publicity we may prefer to avoid. Martha Stewart seems to have survived her well publicized ordeal, appearing in *Martha Stewart Apprentice* about ten minutes after she got out of the Big House. But was the publicity really a "good thing"?

It took comedian Jackie Mason many years to bounce back from purgatory after Ed Sullivan thought Mason gave him "the finger" on the air and banished him.

Tylenol survived the tainted caplets scandal but would they have bounced back if the company hadn't already been well known and respected? I doubt it. Haven't seen Pee Wee Herman around much lately.

Publicity can light a fire for your business. But be sure you're ready to play with matches. Once you put yourself out there in the public arena, you lose a lot of control over what is said about you. But you still have choices to make.

A few years ago, my agent asked if I'd be interested in appearing in a television show, a one-time guest appearance, where I would be seated in one of four corners of a boxing ring, giving my opinion about whatever political topic was thrown out for discussion at the last minute. The show was based on the *Politically Incorrect* model. My initial instinct was to turn it down. What if I said something stupid?

It's better to keep one's mouth shut and be thought a fool than to open it and resolve all doubt.
                                        Abraham Lincoln

And, even if I didn't, how would this enhance my public persona anyway? In deference to my agent, and also to make sure I was not missing a great opportunity, I watched an episode. My initial gut reaction was confirmed; it wasn't for me. It might have made me a little better known, but known for what?

If you're just starting out, turning down publicity oppor-tunities may be the least of your worries. But eventually, if you are doing a fantastic job publicizing yourself, you may find you're spending more time promoting than on your core business.

When to Stop Being Your Own Publicist

This is when you have to start making some choices. It's exciting to be in demand, but make sure that whatever you were so excited about publicizing in the first place isn't getting neglected. At a certain point, you'll have to delegate some of the jobs to others. Hopefully, you will have created such a buzz that you'll need a full-time publicist to take over.

A Star is Born!

There's a showbiz expression — "She's a 10-year overnight success" which refers to paying your dues, playing in two-bit clubs and working your way to the top. And with a handful of exceptions, most stars put in a lot of time and energy to achieve stardom.

That's what publicity is all about. Lots of sweat, organization, constant "list building", M & M's, endless networking, with a ton of creativity, timing and luck thrown in. Success doesn't come overnight, but when it does, you'll forget about all the late nights and stamp lick-ing (just heard a well known marketing guru confess that his cat licked his stamps in the early days!) and just enjoy the glow of the spotlight. And your business will never be the same!

Don't worry if you've gone through this chapter and don't feel ready to publicize yourself yet. Focus on developing a rich authentic persona, crafting a dynamic script and learning how to perform it well. You can pick up this book again when you're ready. Who knows, in the meantime, the media may just come to you.

When you *are* ready, get out there! *Step into the Spotlight!* And don't worry if you encounter a little criticism along the way.

CHAPTER 6

Everybody's A Critic!

THE SHOW MUST GO ON!

*T*he show's over and you're staying up all night to see the review in *Variety* when it comes out at 5:00 A.M. If they pan the show, you'll have to pack up your suitcase and go home to Iowa.

Critics have a tremendous amount of influence, not only in Showbiz but in Regularbiz. "You're Only as Good as Your Last Show" applies with equal vengeance to Business as it does to Show Business. But like a clever sitcom that has to slowly work its way up from last place in the Nielsen ratings, perseverance and a thick skin are key to success.

Stars Must Have a Thick Skin!
....

Stars don't follow trends. They start them!

Which means that, by definition, they're out of fashion for a while. Sometimes a long while. Galileo died before his idea that "the world isn't flat" took hold. Walter Cronkite failed at a local radio audition and was told by the station manager that he'd never make it as an announcer. And Oprah was fired as a television reporter and told "You're not fit for TV."

I heard Jack Canfield say that *Chicken Soup for the Soul* was rejected by 143 publishers who said that no one would buy a book of short stories nowadays. The 144th took a chance on it. Now, entire walls of bookstores are devoted to the 100+ volumes.

In the late 70s, a teenager named Jim and his dad, Percy, took turns on stage at an Open Mike Night of comedy in a dingy basement room of a community center in downtown Toronto, the predecessor of the successful comedy chain Yuk Yuks Komedy Kabaret. According to biographer, Martin Knelman, Percy did OK, but young Jim was given "the hook". The boy couldn't get a laugh and was literally pulled off the stage by a contraption made from a broom handle and a cardboard scythe covered in tinfoil, a "traumatic and humiliating" experience for 14-year-old Jim Carrey. He recovered and went on to earn $10 million for a film appearance.

To be a star, you gotta have a thick skin! Not everyone is going to like you! So, rather than shy away from strong choices, remind yourself that you're not alone.

One of my editors thinks I'm giving too many examples of people who survived their critics. I'm going to give them anyway because they'll give you comfort next time someone slams the door in your face or says "no" or doesn't laugh at your joke. Copy this page and carry it in your wallet for the times you're ready to give up on the spotlight or give up on your dream.

In 1889, the *San Francisco Examiner* sent a letter to Rudyard Kipling (*Jungle Book*) saying:

"I am sorry, Mr. Kipling, but you just do not know how to use the English language."

Margaret Mitchell's *Gone With the Wind* was turned down by over 25 publishers who said "the public is not interested in civil war stories".

Paul McCartney didn't make it into the Liverpool Cathedral Choir. Years later, they commissioned him to write an original cantata.

But it wasn't McCartney's only rejection. He and the rest of the Beatles were rejected by Decca Records in 1962.

In 1865, a review of *Alice in Wonderland* called Lewis Carroll's classic a "stiff silly overwrought story".

Charles Schultz, who created the *Peanuts* comic strip, couldn't even get his stuff into his high school yearbook.

Even Elvis got the "Grand Ole Heave Ho" from the Grand Ole Opry after just one show, the manager telling him: "You ain't going nowhere son. Better get y'all job back drivin' a truck."

Elvis managed to squeak out a bit of a career, in spite of these comments. Many years later, author, Richard Paul Evans, got bumped from a morning TV talk show so that Elvis' pedicurist could come on the show instead, with a jar of Elvis' toenails! (Hook #10)

•   •   •

I think everyone should have a book of these stories on the night table. Pick up a book like *Great Failures of the Extremely Successful* by Steve Young or Harvey Mackay's *We Got Fired... And It's the Best Thing That Ever Happened to Us*. Stars must have a thick skin.

Everybody's a Critic!

Nowadays, we don't even have to wait for the morning paper to print the reviews. Two minutes after an event, we can log onto our computer to see what the world has to say, not just the critics, but the world at large. Recently, I had to replace my 27" Sony TV which had konked out after 14 years of semi-loyal service. As I had done 14 years ago, I checked with the critics, only this time, it wasn't just *Consumer Reports*. I searched for on-line reviews and there were plenty. Ordinary folks, who had bought the TVs, related their stories and graded the TVs on various criteria.

In the face of so much judgment, so much critique, from millions of nameless faceless critics, if you don't have a thick skin, you'll soon opt out of the game. Stars have vision and don't create only for their audiences. While it's true there's no show without an audience, those who attract the spotlight usually create for themselves and allow their audiences to find them.

Another person's opinion is just that, an opinion. When I was leaving law to be a performer, I showed a videotape of me performing to an entertainment lawyer at our firm. I asked for feedback, but I was secretly hoping he'd help connect me. He brought it back and said, "Tsufit, you have a great singing voice, but there's no way you're going to turn that tape into paying work." I thought to myself "Oh yeah?" And it was that tape that got me a week as MC at a comedy club and things took off from there.

Marching to the Beat of Your Own Drum

For about 20 years, I had these oversized 80s style red glasses (Sally Jesse Raphael had nothing on me). When I started my coaching practice, I was constantly told to update my image ("Get with the times!") if I wanted to succeed in my business. Being a hard headed sort, I had fun

with my critics. When I gave speeches, I held up a six foot
long petition that I commissioned my daughter to make,
showing my red glasses crossed out with a red circle
around them (like they do to
indicate "No Smoking") and
teased my audience to sign it.

> A star must
> have vision,
> confidence,
> chutzpah and a
> good set of
> ear plugs!

Finally, because I couldn't
tell the difference between the
postman and a tree, I had to
update my prescription and give
up my beloved specs. I antici-
pated compliments and kudos
from the jury, but instead a new
client asked "What happened to
your funky red glasses? That's
one of the reasons I came to
you." You can't win, so you might as well be yourself.

A star must have vision, confidence, *chutzpah* and a
good set of ear plugs!

Jack Canfield tells a great story about a little boy who
took an "F" on his school story assignment, rather than
change it to be more "realistic" as suggested by his teacher.
The boy had written about a horse ranch he planned to
own someday. While he got an "F" grade on his story,
he got the last laugh, eventually owning the ranch as
planned. The "F" graded paper sits framed above the fire-
place in his 4000 square foot house in the middle of the
200 acre ranch.

Sometimes the "Dream Stealers" mean well. They don't
want you to be disappointed. They think if they criticize
you now, or cut you down to size now, they'll protect you
from the cold cruel world. I know this because I may have
kinda sorta done this to my then eight-year-old daughter,
Aviva, when she announced that she planned to win the

school's public speaking contest. I was afraid she'd come home crying, so I tried to get her to set her sights a little lower. I wanted to protect her from a big let-down. She brought home the medal.

A few years later, my second oldest daughter, Paloma, avenged the crime on her sister. She came home after her school public speaking contest all upset about how someone else won and no one liked her speech, and just as I was shifting gears to move into my "Mommy Comforts Kid on Realities of Cold Cruel World" speech, she laughed "Gotcha! I won!" As you know, eventually all the kids won, so now I just keep my wisdom to myself.

Ultimately, it doesn't really matter if the critics mean well or not. Not sure who said it first, but I love this expression.

Other people's opinions of me are none of my business.

It's damaging to give their input too much weight. That doesn't mean we shouldn't consider what they say — there might be something valuable in it. (I'd be out of business if people didn't consider what I say.) But often the confidence itself creates the success.

Risky Business!
••••••••••••••••••••

In Chapter 4, I encouraged you to use humor in your presentation. But, as you already know, humor is risky business. Johnny Carson once commented that while tragedy affects almost everyone the same way (someone gets hurt, we're all saddened), humor is tricky. Getting the laugh in comedy doesn't only depend on you. You're in the hands of your audience, dependent not only on their mood, but on their points of view.

I remember performing at the Open Mike Night, two nights in a row, at two different locations of Yuk Yuks, the same comedy club where Jim Carrey got thrown off the stage. The first night, I got laughs and thunderous applause. The second night, same material, I couldn't get anyone in the audience to even crack a smile, let alone laugh.

You've gotta have a thick skin. I have a client, a professional speaker, who reconsiders her career choice every time she gets a less than overwhelmingly positive reception. If entertainers quit just because a joke didn't get a laugh, we probably wouldn't have any comedians or singers or motivational speakers today because I doubt very much that there's even one performer in history who hasn't bombed at least once.

Harvey Mackay, in *Beware the Naked Man Who Offers You His Shirt*, quotes a classical composer's response to his critic:

Dear Sir. I am sitting in the smallest room of my house. Your review is before me. Shortly it shall be behind me.
Max Reger

That's a bit extreme.

Invite Your Critics Onto Your Team

While you can't let the critics get to you, it is important to learn from less than stellar performances. Critics can be very valuable, especially if you use them to polish your performance. Despite his harsh delivery, America values Simon Cowell's critical feedback on *American Idol* more than Paula Abdul's gushing.

Boston Philharmonic Conductor, Benjamin Zander, does the unthinkable during his orchestra rehearsals.

As he describes in *The Art of Possibility*, Zander lays to rest the myth of the omniscient conductor by putting "white sheets", blank pieces of paper, on each musician's music stand during each rehearsal and encouraging the musicians to give him feedback on how he's doing as a conductor.

That's the stuff true stars are made of.

If you're really daring and can get over feeling defensive, contacting critics and soliciting further feedback can have huge advantages. Often, you'll win them over (everyone likes to be asked for an opinion) and now they're on you're team. Instead of using their criticism to cut you down, they're going to use it to help sharpen your performance. My experience has been that the people who are inclined to be critics are the same personality types who give raves reviews, *if* you can win them over. They're usually vocal types, so you might as well give it a shot.

Gather Your Allies

Author and speaker, Barbara Sher, has a great idea. She suggests you gather a team of imaginary "allies". Her team includes Golda Meir, Marco Polo, Abraham Lincoln, her grandfather Max and some fictional characters like Shirley Valentine and Jo from *Little Women*. And her "beautiful black dog". These are people (mostly) whom you want in your corner. Each of these allies has a separate voice and a unique perspective to add to yours. You can learn from them and be comforted by them.

Obviously, it helps to have real live allies in your life as well, a nice mix of cheerleaders and people who tell it like it is.

The ear plugs I mentioned earlier — it might be a good idea to take them out once in a while. Even the best can be made better with a little constructive feedback.

I solicit tons of feedback whenever I'm launching something new. I surveyed lots of people about the title of my music CD.

The trick is to ask everyone, listen to everyone, but be selective about what you allow in. You'll need to develop some filters, so that you absorb what's helpful and throw out the rest. Eventually, you'll develop your own panel of judges whose opinions you respect and you'll use their feedback to make your star shine even brighter.

Despite the critics, you *can* be a star!

Ants. Rubbertree plants. Enough said.

CHAPTER 7

Step Into The Spotlight!

LIGHTS, CAMERA, ACTION!
IT'S SHOWTIME!

*W*hen I was a teenager, I appeared in the chorus of the Gilbert and Sullivan operetta *The Gondoliers*. I was also given the honor of being the understudy for Tessa, one of the two female leads. But I never got a chance to rehearse the part and, consequently, I was hugely relieved that the actress never got sick. I wasn't prepared to step onto the stage in her place. Years later, I still have nightmares about being called to go on stage and not knowing my lines...

Remember what the Boy Scouts say? "Be prepared." I say, "Wear a belt and suspenders and a helmet. But then, jump G-ddammit, jump!"

> *Get off the couch!*
> Lord Chesterfield

OK, so maybe Lord Chesterfield (real guy) didn't exactly say that. But *I'm* saying it.

It's time. No more fooling around.

Take Center Stage
••••••••••••••••••••••••

Take it. No one's going to hand it to you.

Take a Risk. Step into the Spotlight!
••

Years ago, when I was seriously pregnant (when wasn't I?), trying to kill time till the kid popped out, I went to The Second City in downtown Toronto to see a show. I got into a conversation with the theater's ticket taker, a nice girl named Nia. We told each other that we were both actresses waiting for our big break and we exchanged phone numbers. All I can remember about her is that she had this cute perky 50s high ponytail on one side of her head.

Years later, I read in one of those free movie magazines that one night, a Second City actress fell ill right before a show. The ticket taker on duty that night took a risk and told the director, "I know all her lines. Let me go on." And in desperation, they did. The risk paid off. She got hired the next day!

The ticket girl I met all those years ago was Nia Vardalos, the writer and star of *My Big Fat Greek Wedding*, a hugely successful independently made movie.

It's not enough to learn how to step into the spotlight. You actually have to *do* it. You actually have to take the step.

You Don't Have to Wait

And you don't have to wait to be invited into the spotlight. Use the techniques in Chapters 3, 4 and 5 to be ready to take center stage and be a star wherever you go. You never know when an opportunity will present itself.

Access Your "Inner *Chutzpah*"

Stars don't usually become stars by chance. I recently heard *New York Times* best-selling author, Richard Paul Evans tell the story of how he stepped into the spotlight.

Earlier in his career, when his book, *The Christmas Box*, wasn't doing well nationally, Evans forked over $500, a huge sum for him at the time, for a booth at a trade show in Denver, Colorado. His goal was to connect with booksellers, but he soon became frustrated. His booth wasn't getting any traffic because all the booksellers were in another room, lining up in front of a table on a platform where a panel of best-selling authors was auto-graphing books.

"Take the Seat!"

Evans looked enviously at those authors and was about to leave in frustration, when he noticed one empty chair at the table on the platform. Although he says it wasn't easy for him to do, this shy guy somehow accessed his "inner *chutzpah*" and walked straight onto the platform, sat in the empty spot between two best-selling authors and started signing books like he was meant to be there all along. The following year, he returned as the headliner, the premier best-selling author of the event. Evans' advice? "Take the Seat!"

All the World's a Stage
....

It's not always that dramatic. You can create a stage wherever you go. When I turn it "on", that's where the stage is. How do you do that?

Be Electric!
....

It takes energy, electricity, to seduce the spotlight.

You need to be "on" like a light bulb. I remember Sister Anne (the real life nun who directed our production of *The Sound of Music* when I was 15) scolding me in rehearsal: "Tsufit, you look like a piece of limp spaghetti up there!"

Spaghetti doesn't cut it on stage. When you're "on", you can feel the energy in your arms and radiating all around you. Your audience can feel it from the third balcony. I'm not talking "stick your finger in the light socket, hair stand up on end" energy. It's an intensity in your voice, your stance, in the way you hold your head and most of all in your eyes.

Plugging Yourself In
....

You don't have to be loud. As I said, noise is the first thing that gets filtered out. Tracy Chapman wrote a song about how a revolution starts "with a whisper". A whisper can be very intense.

I'd like to say that this intensity comes from a belief in your message and letting your passion shine through, and certainly that's part of it. But some people have the talent of being captivating when talking about dog food. We all have this internal energy; we just have to learn to tap into it.

Tony Robbins says that our choice of words and how we hold our bodies makes a huge difference, not only in how we appear to others, but how we feel ourselves.

He's right. Often, it happens naturally, when we get excited about something, but you can learn to put yourself in that state of excitement.

It's Showtime!

Performers have no choice. I've had to step onto the stage five minutes after having an argument. It's interesting to watch performers "flip the switch" on TV shows like *Last Comic Standing*. You can see the performer backstage (serious, tense and focused) and then running onto stage with a big fat smile, loose and ready to roll.

"Quiet On The Set!"

You have to leave everything else that's going on in your life off stage and get focused. I make sure that I'm completely alone for five minutes before I hit the stage and I try to make that a quiet time. It helps me get mentally ready for the spotlight. Football teams do the huddle. So do some musicians and theater troupes. Sometimes, they even throw in a quick pray.

Get Ready to Flip the Switch

Now you're ready for "Action"! A couple of ideas to get you into that electric state. Physical movement, jumping up and down or running helps. My voice teacher used to make me do jumping jacks before singing to "oxygenate" my voice. And don't forget the music. Crank it up on your headphones and dance around for a few minutes before you're on.

Yeah, I know I just said "quiet time". Works for me, but some people need to get revved up just before they hit the stage. Or try the "Quiet Then Crank" Combo, focus then get pumped.

Leave 'em Wanting More

Word of warning. You can't be "on" all the time. You can't live your whole life in the spotlight. It's exhausting. Being "on" burns calories, just like running a marathon or getting a workout at the gym. After you walk off stage, you're hungry, ravenous, like after sex.

I guess some celebrities manage to do it, but I think the price is too high. Even a light bulb burns out if left on all the time. You need to learn to step out of the spotlight to recharge your batteries. And then, quickly, jump back in.

Don't Be Afraid to Say "No" to the Spotlight

Like an Oscar-winning actress who reads 100 scripts for every movie she does, anyone who's going for star status should be discerning and consider every opportunity carefully.

I decline almost as many invitations into the spotlight as I accept. I've turned down comedy gigs, keynote speeches, my solo in a musical because it was in too high a key — I scrutinize each opportunity and ask myself whether it will get me my star outside Grauman's Chinese Theater or not. And even if it will, I ask myself if that's still what I want. On the other hand, you never know which invitation will lead to your "big break". The Chicken Soup duo agreed early on to each do 5 things every day to promote their book and look how that turned out.

Building Momentum
....

Just like getting a plane off the ground, you'll need an initial push to get yourself into the air.

When I started my business, I worked furiously day and night, despite family suggestions to slow down. I understood, intuitively, what I now know to be a fact. Slow and steady does *not* win this race! You have to get in the air first and then you can be steady. But steady doesn't get you launched. You just have to jump off and go for it!

OK, let's get ready for takeoff.

The Seven Steps to Stardom
....

1. Develop and define your persona, your role.
2. Figure out what you're really selling.
3. Dig for your story add some color.
4. Connect your story to what you're selling.
5. Figure out what to say and how to say it.
6. Access your "Inner *Chutzpah*".
7. Go for it! Step into the Spotlight!

Notice, I didn't add publicity to the seven steps. Publicity is optional. It's not for everybody. If you're ready to put in the sweat equity to accelerate your success, publicity is definitely the way to go. It can exponentially increase your visibility and credibility. But it's not for everybody. And you can get there without it. (Truth? I wanted the alliteration of "seven steps to stardom" and I ran out of numbers.)

If you've read this whole book and followed the steps and something still doesn't feel right, you have one more question to ask yourself.

Are You in the Right Business?

It's hard to star in your business if you're in the wrong business.

Remember my first law job? The one where they created that extra position for me. Since they were only planning to hire one lawyer, they had only one office, so for a couple of months, the other new lawyer and I shared an office while they built an extra office for me.

One night, she came to see me perform in a show. The next day, she said to me, "Tsufit, I can't believe that person on stage is the person I share an office with. I see you every day. But on stage, you're a totally different person. You have the audience eating out of your hands!"

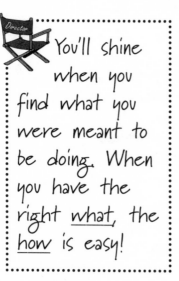

You'll shine when you find what you were meant to be doing. When you have the right _what_, the _how_ is easy!

Maybe law wasn't the right business for me. Maybe that's not what I was meant to be doing.

Sometimes clients come to me for help with their marketing and I quickly realize that they're not passionate about what they're doing.

It's hard to promote that. It's hard to shine. You'll shine when you find what you were meant to be doing. When you have the right "what", the "how" is easy!

Comedienne, Paula Poundstone, says that adults are always asking kids what they want to be when they grow up because they're looking for ideas.

Have Fun!

. . . .

I'd like to quote one of my favorite 20th century philosophers, Poppins (maybe you've heard of her?), Mary:

> With every job that must be done, there is an element of fun. You find the fun and snap the job's a game.

If you're not having fun, fuggedaboutit!!! And the bonus is: fun sells!

If you're not having fun, fuggedaboutit!!!
And the bonus is: fun sells!
When you find what you love to do, that's when your color will shine through!
That's when you'll star in your own business!
You'll be a magnet. You'll attract!
And there'll be no stopping you!

•••

One last word. This, I learned both as a performer on stage and as a lawyer in court.

You gotta know when to sit down and shut up!

Curtain

COOL MARKETING BLOGS

Advergirl	leighhouse.typepad.com/advergirl
Blogging Me Blogging You	bloggingmebloggingyou.wordpress.com
Brand Autopsy	brandautopsy.com
Branding & Marketing	brandandmarket.blogspot.com
Buzz Canuck	buzzcanuck.typepad.com
Canuckflack	canuckflack.com
Church of the Customer	churchofthecustomer.com
Common Sense PR	www.commonsensepr.com
Communication Overtones	overtonecomm.blogspot.com
ConverStations	www.converstations.com
Copyblogger	copyblogger.com
Customers Rock!	customersrock.wordpress.com
Diva Marketing Blog	divamarketingblog.com
Drew's Marketing Minute	www.drewsmarketingminute.com
Duct Tape Marketing	www.ducttapemarketing.com
Experience Manifesto	blog.brandexperiencelab.org
Golden Practices	goldenmarketing.typepad.com
Idea Sellers	ideaseller.typepad.com
Logic+Emotion	darmano.typepad.com
Marketing Monster	marketingmonster.wordpress.com
Marketing Pilgrim	marketingpilgrim.com
mindblob	mindblob.typepad.com
Personal Branding Blog	personalbrandingblog.wordpress.com
PR Squared	www.pr-squared.com
PR Works	www.prworks.ca
Servant of Chaos	servantofchaos.typepad.com
Seth's Blog	sethgodin.typepad.com
StickyFigure	www.stickyfigure.com
Strategic Public Relations	prblog.typepad.com
Techno//Marketer	technomarketer.typepad.com
the brand builder blog	thebrandbuilder.blogspot.com
The Engaging Brand	theengagingbrand.typepad.com
The Idea Grove	ideagrove.com
The Lonely Marketer	www.lonelymarketer.com
tompeters!	www.tompeters.com
Transmission Content + Creative	transmissionmarketing.ca
Two Hat Marketing	www.twohatmarketing.com
Web Ink Now	www.webinknow.com
whatsnextblog.com	www.whatsnextblog.com

More great marketing blogs at www.power150.com

INDEX

About The Author

After 10 years as a Dean's List litigation lawyer, TSUFIT left law for the limelight, performing comedy on national television and gaining international attention for her debut music CD. Tsufit is now a marketing consultant who coaches entrepreneurs and CEOs to be stars. A popular radio & television show guest, keynote speaker, seminar leader and mom, Tsufit points out that she is not taking on any more clients in the last category!

Visit Tsufit at www.tsufit.com.

ACKNOWLEDGEMENTS

Thank you to a fantastic team of editors, Joan Homewood and Karen Opas and to Cathy Leek who became so much more than an editor to me.

Thank you to Heidy Lawrance, who is not only great at what she does, but a sweetheart to boot. Thanks also to Heidy's design team.

Thanks also to my advance readers and fellow entrepreneurs and to the many booksellers who gave insightful feedback. And thanks to the people of New York City and Toronto (I spoke to most of them!) for answering my impromptu surveys in bookstores, parks and shared taxi cabs.

And to the awe-inspiring authors and industry leaders who endorsed this book — I'm honored by your kind words and grateful for your encouragement and support. Your books are the ones I have in my personal library. What a thrill to have your words on my book!

Thanks to David Chilton and to Spencer Gale for your support and advice and a special thanks to the magnificent Sheldon Bowles. Thanks to Meg and Todd and all the amazing bloggers who are helping spread the word. And to Dottie — you will be missed.

Thank you to my amazing daughters, who brought me food when I refused to leave my desk for days on end and served as a second team of top notch editors. You rock!

And to my parents, my dad who's a star in front of a crowd and my mom who gets rave reviews from everyone she charms one-on-one, I thank you, in advance, for the feedback I'm about to receive, when I give you a copy of this book.

275

SEND IN YOUR STORIES!

You've heard my stories. Now, I'd love to hear yours.

So, send me your stories of stepping into the spotlight, what worked, what didn't, anything funny or amusing that happened along the way and any success stories that resulted from reading this book. Include your full contact information (postal address, e-mail, telephone number) and any questions you'd like to see answered in my next book. But don't tell me any secrets. Who knows? I just might share them with the whole world in my next project, so please only send stories that you are granting me permission to publish.

Send your stories to: story@tsufit.com

With the subject line: "Stories From The Spotlight!" from [Your Name].

Until then...
See You in the Spotlight!

Tsufit